BUSINESS
OWNERSHIP
A SURVIVAL GUIDE

THE JOY.

THE PAIN.

THE TRUTH.

Foreword by Adam Bryant, Managing Director Merryck & Co.
Former *Corner Office* Columnist for *The New York Times*

"If people wanted to be written about more warmly, they should have behaved better."

– Anne Lamott

For David Bohan and John Sharpe,
who believed I could and told me so.

For Bill Breen who gave me
a vision of what could be.

For Jack Paramore, my foundation.

And for Vera, my reason.

Cover Design: Julie Allen
Interior Design: Dino Marino, www.mybook.design

Hardback ISBN: 978-1-7343386-2-1
Paperback ISBN: 978-1-7343386-3-8
eBook ISBN: 978-1-7343386-0-7

WELCOME TO THE WORLD OF
BUSINESS OWNERSHIP

This book is just the beginning, even though I wrote it at the end of my time as the owner of Paramore Digital. I learned hundreds of lessons about building and running a business. Many of those I've shared on my website at hannahparamore.com. I hope you'll become a regular reader of the blog there and leave your comments. I'll learn from you!

Every month I share my thoughts about business ownership and the joys and challenges inherent to it through a newsletter. If you'll join that newsletter, I'll send you an unpublished piece of gold titled "Structure Works." It'll help you think through how to build your team specifically to get the most out of your talented group.

Go to HannahParamore.com/the-book and sign up at the bottom of the page.

Connect to me at:
Linkedin.com/hp
Facebook.com/hannahparamore
Instagram.com/hannahparamore59
Email: Hannah@hannahparamore.com

Join the conversation at BusinessOwnership-TheBook.com

TABLE OF CONTENTS

FOREWORD

There is too much happy talk in business.

Ask any entrepreneur how their company is doing, and you're likely to hear, "Everything's great, we're killing it." It's not true, of course, and even sharp growth carries with it an inevitable host of problems. But business owners understandably want to exude confidence for their customers, clients and investors, and to create that pixie-dust aura that they're building something special. As a result, though, entrepreneurship often can seem like it's part of an Instagram #BestLife feed, exacerbating the loneliness of leading a business and making entrepreneurs wonder at times, "Is it just me who has these problems?"

Thankfully, Hannah Paramore Breen has written a much-needed gut-check on what the life of an entrepreneur is really like.

I first met Hannah in 2014, when I interviewed her for my Corner Office series in The New York Times. The idea behind that series, in which I interviewed more than 500 CEOs over a decade, was to never ask any of them about their company's strategy or industry, and instead ask them about the most important leadership lessons they had learned. Hannah shared powerful stories of her early years, including the strong work ethic instilled by her family, and the many setbacks she faced that tested her resilience and perseverance as she forged her own path. We stayed in touch after our interview, sharing a meal on occasion when she was in New York. We talked about life and business, and her company seemed to be on a smooth and steady trajectory.

Then in 2016, she called me with the news: she had sold Paramore Digital, the company she had built from scratch and that had her name above the door (and on the building that is home to its Nashville headquarters). I confess that I was surprised. After all, her firm seemed to be perfectly positioned to surf the digital wave transforming every business and industry, and she has a big, energetic personality — always helpful in an industry where personal connections matter. As I've spent more time in Nashville, where our youngest daughter now lives, I've come to understand that she is the unofficial mayor of the city. Hannah knows *everybody*. Why would she want to sell? On that call, she talked about it being the right time, and wanting to start a new chapter.

But now, thankfully, we have the fuller answer about why Hannah sold Paramore Digital, and the book you are holding should be required reading for anyone who either wants to start a business or who already owns a business and wonders why problems only seem to multiply, especially ones that involve human beings. Brace yourself, though. Hannah has spared the Novocain in this candid look at the life of an entrepreneur. A natural story-teller, Hannah shares vivid tales that capture the many maddening paradoxes and infuriating realities of building and running a business, including the fact that you are losing even as you are winning, that the strengths of a young and energetic team can also be weaknesses, and that loyalty is often a one-way street. Anybody who is on the fence about whether they want to start a business won't be after they finish this book.

If you're looking for more of a fist-pumping, you-can-do-it inspirational book, there are plenty of options out there already for you. But if you are truly determined to start your own business, I would argue that you don't need those books. There is no deterring a real entrepreneur, because their particular mix of motivation is so powerful — an idea that consumes them, the drive to create and build something, the resolve to strike out on their own because they can't stomach working for another bad boss — that they don't need a rah-rah book.

For any entrepreneur, first-timer or veteran, this book is filled with the most valuable kind of advice: lessons, insights and stories from someone with hard-earned experience and wisdom to share. An entrepreneur's life is a roller coaster ride, often with many highs and lows packed into the same day. So, enjoy the fleeting highs, and then reach for this book when you hit the inevitable lows. Hannah will remind you that it's not just you. Employees can be impossible. Clients can be exasperating. You will be living an endless game of Whack-a-Mole, with new problems popping up the minute you solve others.

Keep Hannah's book by your bed. At the end of a horrible day, she's the friend who understands what you're going through, because she's been there herself. And she can share some tips and insights on how to tackle the challenges tomorrow, when you wake up and get back on the roller-coaster ride of building your business. Because that's what entrepreneurs, with their laudable superpowers of perseverance and resilience, do: they get up and go after it, day after day after day, until the day comes when it's time to move on.

— Adam Bryant, Managing Director, Merryck & Co.,
Former "Corner Office" Columnist
for the *New York Times*

INTRODUCTION

This is a story about loss.

In 2002, I lost my fourth job in two years and decided that was a crazy way to earn a living. I'd been in the digital industry for six years, riding the wave of the dot-com bubble as it peaked and then crashed. After a three-year stint at CitySearch.com, I took one job after another so I could both stay in the industry and stay in Nashville. Each position went bust after just a handful of months for various reasons, but I wasn't too worried about it at the time because every time I'd get a new job, I'd get a $20,000 increase in pay. Not bad.

When I realized that the people who were trying to recruit me should actually be working for me, I decided to stop the madness and go out on my own. I took a small consulting project with the National Federation of Independent Business (NFIB), helping them develop a website for their Human Resources department. As an extension of that first contract, I helped them simplify their recruiting materials, creating a CD that would replace the VHS tape and 8.5x11-inch folder full of hiring documents that had been so cumbersome and expensive for them to assemble and mail to the 3,000 inquiries they got every year.

It was a cool project. When I got the boxes full of 2,500 CDs—all neat and tidy and shrink-wrapped and brand consistent—I was a little giddy. I was ushering in a new age for this stalwart organization that represented small businesses across the country!

Standing in my home office, surrounded by boxes of CDs, I admired the packaging and the beautiful artwork. I turned one over and ran my hand over the clean, white back, tracing the address and phone number of the home office, located in Nashville and wondered, "Who answers this 800 number when you call it?"

I picked up my office phone and dialed the number, which was answered by a sex-talk recording. "Press 1 if you are interested in …"

It was an auspicious beginning to what would become a flourishing business—my business.

Within two weeks after signing that first contract, I had four more clients. Altogether, their billing totaled more money than I'd ever made in corporate America.

For fifteen years, I owned and ran and loved my company, Paramore Digital. We became a premier digital agency in the early days of the industry. Over those fifteen years, we had marquee clients both in Nashville and across the country. We built big websites, ran digital media campaigns, created content for the web, and built web and smartphone apps. And we had so much fun.

I learned more about myself, about life, and about people by owning a company than through any other endeavor in my life. I made lasting friends. I traveled the world. I made a lot of money. And then I sold it.

Everybody was surprised that I sold the business. From the outside, we were nothing but successful by every measure. Our work won every award imaginable. We were in the Inc. 5,000 list of fastest-growing companies in the U.S. and Nashville's Future 50 list for five straight years, entering the Hall of Fame for both at the same time. We were one of Nashville's top fifteen women-owned businesses for a long time. I was a finalist for the CEO of the Year in 2012 and 2013 in Nashville and a Woman of Influence in 2009. We were voted one of the Best Places to Work many times. I spoke at major conferences internationally. We received international press in places like *Business Insider, Businessweek, Fast Company, Success Magazine, The WSJ* and the granddaddy of them all, *The New York Times*.

And yet, in the middle of the success, my days were full of anxiety and loss. As a business owner, even while you are winning in so many ways, you are also losing. Business ownership is a process of continual shedding. Over the years, those losses mount up to a point that your outlook on the future path of the business becomes cloudy. It is hard to see a way forward that isn't full of more pain.

Such is the way of life. In a grand example of Newton's third law of motion, for every moment of a business owner's joy, there is an equal and opposite moment of pain.

BUSINESS OWNERSHIP IS A PROCESS OF CONTINUAL SHEDDING.

I wish I had known that along the way. Although I had good mentors and coaches who meant a lot to me, I never had another business owner tell me the truth about what they were enduring and their struggles dealing with the highs and lows of owning a business.

The struggle is real.

During a personal time of struggle, I read II Corinthians 1 with new eyes: "Blessed be the God and Father of our Lord Jesus Christ, the Father of mercies and God of all comfort, who comforts us in all our tribulation, that we may be able to comfort those who are in trouble with the comfort with which we ourselves are comforted by God."

In other words, pay it forward. Do something good with your pain.

Although I'd been reading the Bible since I was young, I didn't remember ever reading this section, and I pondered it. Just a few days later, I went to the church I'd been attending. Although I attended fairly regularly, only one of the pastors, Bert Thompson, knew my name. We had spoken briefly only twice in the previous several months.

He didn't know anything about my personal or professional life. That morning, he was seated directly in front of me, and, at the end of the service, he turned around and said, "I believe I have a specific word for you. The scripture says that God is the God of all comforts…"

I picked it up, "…who comforts us in all our tribulation, that we may be able to comfort those who are in trouble…"

He said, "How do you know this scripture?"

I said, "How are you saying this to me right now?"

They call those "God winks."

For the last few years that I owned Paramore Digital, the greatest question I wrestled with was, "What am I supposed to do with what I've built?" Was there a right answer to this great question, or was it just completely up to my whim? How would I know when the right answer was staring me in the face?

If you are reading this book, I'll bet you have the same question. So I am paying it forward. I am doing something good with my pain. I hope that as you read this book, you will find help, support, and comfort, along with some ideas that will help you know what to do with what you've built.

— CHAPTER ONE —

AMBIEN DAY

I took Ambien in the office one day. Not on purpose. I meant to take a Xanax.

I don't remember as much of the three-hour conference call that followed as my team does. It seems that some of it was downright comical. What is impressive, at least to me, is that although I was slurring my words and leaving the office mid-sentence, the team said I remained engaged in the discussion. Every time someone recommended we take this up later, I'd say, "No, we are going to do this right now," and slam my hand down on the desk.

Somehow, I stayed upright throughout the day and apparently made two phone calls, as I would soon find out. I met my boyfriend, Bill, as well as his mother and his two uncles, both Catholic priests, for dinner. I had two glasses of wine, went home, took another Ambien, and had the best sleep of my life.

I was *soooo* rested the next morning. Happy as a lark.

When Bill left to give golf lessons, I jumped on the grid and found a text and a voicemail awaiting me. Both were from concerned friends asking if I was, umm, *all right* after yesterday.

Blank.

I was just about to return one call when I reached into my purse for my pen—I cannot work without a pen in my hand—and pulled out the bag that contained my new Xanax prescription, stapled shut.

No way. How could that be? I'd taken one yesterday, right? I definitely took *something…*

For years, I'd taken Ambien every night because my mind won't slow down. My theory at the time was: keep your Ambien in your purse because you never know where you're going to sleep.

I fumbled around in my purse to find the bottle, checked the refill date, and counted pills. Yep, one short.

I started to sweat as blurry snatches of memory began to resurface.

On my cell phone, my back to the door…

"Dan, how can I get out of the office lease?"

"John, we lost our biggest client. I'll have to lose people. Clients suck."

Walking out of the office as Sheri called behind me, "Hannah, sit down; let me get what you need."

Slurring my words as Blake tilted his head and leaned forward.

It was August of 2015, and we were closing out our thirteenth profitable year in a dynamic industry full of young, talented people. We were well-positioned. We had a reputation for doing what we said we would do. We were disciplined and creative.

We also threw great parties. I had a rock show as a birthday party for years. Open bar, everyone invited. We called our client trips "honeymoons." We had two ping pong tables, a cornhole game set, a basketball goal, a disco ball, and good music in the office. We took annual planning retreats reminiscent of church camp.

I was pretty well-known in the city, too. I had an international network and had been featured in *The New York Times, Fast Company, Inc., Business Insider,* and more. The sign on the top of our building had my name on it, and we had a rooftop deck on the best corner downtown. I'm not bragging. I'm trying to say that I had a good life. I had all of the things my preacher said are necessary for happiness: someone to love, something to do, and something to look forward to.

So why was I pill-popping in the middle of the day?

There were many things that could have made that happen over the previous thirteen years: alcoholic partner, a break with another key relationship, trouble at home. But on this day, it was the unexpected loss of our largest client for the second time in two years. We had not replaced the first major client loss, so this one put our company at risk. All indications from the client had been that our relationship would grow through an RFP process after five years of unprecedented success, so we were scaling up. Clearly, we did not really know what was going on.

What I did know on that day was that we were facing the worst: a severe drop in revenue, staff reduction, and quite possibly the end.

We had been through the loss of a major client twice in our history, once during the economic downturn of 2008-2011. Although I was stressed in those times too, it never felt insurmountable to me. And that is odd, considering that during one of those losses, I also fired and divorced my husband on the same day, which meant that I owed him a lot of money. But this time felt different. I was panicked.

What unfolded over the twelve months following Ambien Day is both painful and wonderful. The punchline is not a surprise: I sold my business.

What is a surprise is *why* I sold it.

I was forty-two years old when I started Paramore. I had a feeling of freedom, of crossing over to the other side, where I belonged. I was an accidental entrepreneur, which isn't all that uncommon, as it turns out. I had great confidence in my ability to make a difference for my clients, to make good decisions, to run a business well. The community was supportive; Nashville is a great place to start a business.

For the first nine years, we almost never lost. There was normal client churn and normal employee turnover, but we won almost everything we pitched. We were growing 30-50 percent each year. Almost every day was a kick. The industry was new, and we were in a mid-sized market, so people with experience in digital were rare. We were making it up as we went along.

I did not have a clear model for a digital agency, because I didn't know that's what I was starting. Although I'd been in marketing for a while, I'd never actually worked for an agency. I also wasn't certain I'd be on my own for long, so there was no grand plan. I just started working, and one thing led to another. You can do that when the industry is young, until something transpires and you can't answer the question, "Why is this happening?"

A successful business is part expertise, part opportunity, and part inspiration. Which of those is most important depends on the type of business you own. In my case, as it turns out, inspiration was the motivating factor for Paramore Digital. I am an inspirational leader. I lean on my powers of persuasion and the ability to inspire people to trust me. My business coach once told me that whichever direction I decided the room was going, that's where the room went.

I had a great model. When I was a child, my father was a preacher. We revered him. He is the reason I listen with rapt attention to the speaker in the room. He taught me to weave a story with an emotional ending, to respect the space between words.

The scripture was written on the doorposts of our house and tacked on the bulletin board in our den with word pictures called flannelgraph. It was my mother who taught me Ecclesiastes 9:10: "Whatever your hand finds to do, do it with all your might."

When I could no longer do that, it was time to sell the company.

But why could I no longer do that when *my name was on the building?*

In retrospect, I realize it started with a single question triggered by a change I saw during the recession. It was late hitting us, but when it did, I asked, "How do I know when I need to hire somebody?" Years earlier, I'd realized that our growth was only limited by the number of people we had on staff. People equal capacity in our business. And it worked for a good, long time. It stopped working sometime around 2010.

The deeper I got into that, the more another question rattled in my head: "Is the industry pivoting?"

And then another: "How will I keep from missing the next pivot?"

And finally, "What do I do when we've reached a point where we can't rebound?"

I chased those questions through processes and people, trying desperately to see the future. I listened to consultants, joined peer groups, and read books that told me to give more power to my already-empowered team.

And then Ambien Day happened, followed by twelve months of introspection.

After fourteen straight years of profitable business and

perceived control over my destiny, the thought that I could not put aside in the months leading up to the acquisition was this:

We don't really know what's going on.

In fact, the amount that we don't know about any aspect of our lives is astounding. We didn't really know what was happening with our clients. I didn't know what the Paramore team wanted or what really motivated them. We often don't know what's going on with our spouse or our children. We're lucky if we know what's going on inside ourselves.

Selling a business is hard. The due diligence process is torture. It focuses only on the black-and-white facts of your business, not the shadows and color of the love and experiences and impact you've had.

Deciding to sell your business is even harder. It is an emotional process caused by the painful journey of business ownership.

> SELLING A BUSINESS IS HARD. THE DUE DILIGENCE PROCESS IS TORTURE. IT FOCUSES ONLY ON THE BLACK-AND-WHITE FACTS OF YOUR BUSINESS, NOT THE SHADOWS AND COLOR OF THE LOVE AND EXPERIENCES AND IMPACT YOU'VE HAD.

Now, just barely on the other side, I am looking back on the last fifteen years and what strikes me is that I know there was success, but all I can feel is the loss.

> **DECIDING TO SELL YOUR BUSINESS IS EVEN HARDER. IT IS AN EMOTIONAL PROCESS CAUSED BY THE PAINFUL JOURNEY OF BUSINESS OWNERSHIP.**

Upon reflection, I see specific pivot points in the business that changed me one piece at a time and lessened my enjoyment of it. Most of them have to do with the loss of people. Whether the end result of a business is a successful sale or not, you become willing to part with something you've built through a series of painful events.

Loss creates an opening.

For three years, I struggled with what to do with the business. When you ask someone to advise you on whether or not you should sell your business, they will not answer your question. It all depends on you, just like everything else always has. And yet for all the world, I wanted somebody to tell me what to do.

I was raised with a strong sense of personal responsibility. When I was a teenager, things fell apart for my family, leaving us all stunned—and me in charge of my father and younger sister. I struggled with that for so long. After the loss of our biggest client in 2014, in an emotional meeting with my business coach, I found myself talking to her about that old pain and she said to me, "If you could go back to that time, what is the question you would ask of your parents, who were supposed to be taking care of you?"

I thought of that broken-hearted seventeen-year-old and said, "What am I supposed to do now?"

"And if you could give them the answer, what would it be?" she asked.

And I barely whispered, "Help me."

That is the way I felt on Ambien Day.

Writing this has been hard, like looking at photos of a lost love or a previous life. I've had to remember the good, which makes me melancholy, and the bad, which makes me sad.

Like everything in your life that is worth something, the answer to the following question is intensely personal, but I'm going to share my experience with you to help you answer the question, "Why would you sell a business with your name on it?"

Here's why.

— CHAPTER TWO —

THE STAFF
A STRENGTH TAKEN TOO FAR

A few years into the business, I was having dinner with a client, talking about the work we were doing together, when he shifted the conversation a bit.

"You have a nice business, Hannah. But what are you going to do with it?"

I was immediately defensive. My answer was something like, "I'm doing it. Running it. What do you mean?"

"There is one problem with your business," he said. "It's a people business. I hope that doesn't offend you."

Blank stare. "What do you mean?"

"Look, the people you hire are young, and they are needy. They depend on you too much. Before long, they will drive you crazy with their demands, and it's just going to get worse as time goes on. They will strip everything from you. You should sell it now, while you're on the way up. Create a business that generates passive income, where you don't have to deal with people."

I was offended; I couldn't imagine anything worse. After years spent just working to provide, I was having the time of my life creating a company and leading a team. I'm good with people. I get energy from people. People are everything, aren't they? Since he was my client, I'd seen this guy in action. He was successful by force, not because he was admired as an effective leader. So, considering the source, I dismissed his comments.

He was the first to put it out there so plainly, but he was not the first to try to tell me how hard it would be to grow a business that was dependent on a group of young, creative people. Others had made more subtle insinuations about the flip side of starting a company. After the compliment for taking the risk and supporting multiple families through my fledgling business, they would grimace and say something like, "but the *people*…" and trail off. I barely heard them.

At the time, we had about fifteen people on the team, and so far, it had been great. Turnover was low. After just seven years in business, we had several employees who had passed the five-year mark already. The energy was good, and so was our work. We won awards. We won most of the business we pitched. Thoughts of failure or even big challenges never entered my mind. We were already more successful than I'd ever thought we would be.

I had not planned to grow the company to a specific

size. In fact, I had not planned on it being a company at all. After finding my niche in digital in the late '90s, I'd gone through the tough years of the first dot-com bust when even good internet companies couldn't stay in business. Jobs disappeared overnight - including mine. Repeatedly. I was a single mother of two teenagers, so I wasn't able to relocate to a major market where the only digital jobs still remained and where the industry was advancing despite the hiccup in 2001. I desperately wanted to stay in the industry, so I started consulting, with no expectation that it would last and no plans for it to be anything more.

Fortunately for me, Nashville was small, so once the word was out that I was consulting, my phone started to ring. A handful of months later, it was a client who noticed I needed some help. He suggested I hire Carrie, who was transitioning from an agency job and willing to work part-time with no strings.

Carrie knew things I didn't know, like what a "change order" was. I had never worked for an agency, so it was all a mystery to me, and Carrie was a blessing. I hardly ever saw her. We'd meet in a coffee shop once a week or so, which was enough because I didn't really know how to use her. Mostly I just nodded my head to every suggestion she'd make about what she could do with her time. I didn't think I could afford to keep her on when she finally said she needed to make a minimum of $1,000 per month to continue working with me and pass up a job as a receptionist for Alan Jackson (yes, the singer; I do live in Nashville, remember...). I couldn't imagine losing her by that time, so I ponied up and she came along for the ride.

During those first years, I learned that I am a finisher by nature, so consulting in this new industry was frustrating for me. It wasn't enough to talk to somebody about a solution; I wanted to settle on the solution and then see it working. Since I am a strategist, not a designer or developer, that meant I had to hire people to produce the work.

It also meant I needed an office, because I don't really like coffee shops.

David Bohan, the Founder and then CEO of bohan, an advertising and marketing agency in Nashville, became my first mentor. Taking as gospel his wisdom that your company can't outgrow your real estate, we rented space in the same building as his agency and shared the space with another small company for the first year. Things moved fast from there. I would look out my office window at the Nashville skyline and see nothing but opportunity. Then I would look back at our staff of four and see panic. The opportunity out there was far greater than the staff could handle. But the thought of hiring made me sweat. Making commitments like that in an industry where the workload shifts quickly and dramatically felt risky. How would I know if I could pay them next month?

I should have learned it sooner, but it took me a while to realize that in a custom creative services company, the only inventory you have is the number of hours you can work. Hours equal people. More people equal more inventory, so as long as you have enough business, people are not an expense; they are capacity.

Once I learned that, my mentality shifted to hire, hire, hire. My hiring strategy was based on gut. There was nothing scientific about it, and we did not have a process. We just met people, offered them a job and bought them a MacBook, grateful they accepted a job at a company with no structure, no job descriptions, and few benefits.

I thought my negative client was wrong. The business continued to grow despite the warning he gave me over dinner. I put it out of my mind, kept my head down, and worked.

And it did work. For years, every time we hired people, our revenue increased.

And then, seemingly overnight, it didn't.

I looked up one day to catch a glimpse of the first flyby. We'd never had an employee come and go in less time than it took me to learn his name. He wasn't the last.

I looked down to see the numbers going in opposite directions. Operating costs were up. Revenue was flat. Profit was down.

I looked outside for answers.

I looked inside for mistakes.

What just happened?!

WHAT JUST HAPPENED

What just happened was the first indication that turnover would become a problem, which was particularly frustrating for me because we had such a great thing going on. Our office was in the trendy district in downtown Nashville, in a renovated industrial building. It was an open-office style, which made for a relaxed, transparent environment. We had expanded from three to about twenty people, and we were very hip.

We were a celebration-oriented company, so our culture developed naturally. We were working hard to create something in a brand-new industry, just following the opportunity. There were few standards and fewer rules. Most people on the team were young and single. Friendships developed. So did traditions.

For example, we wore formal wear every Leap Day and took company retreats every October. On the first Formal Wear Day, which fell on a Wednesday in 2012, I wore my first wedding dress—complete with a cathedral train and a fingertip veil—all day long. I put it on at my house and wore it while driving to work, putting my time in at the office, and walking to a Mexican restaurant for lunch. That night at home, I had a panic attack when I couldn't unzip it (I lived alone).

Having fun together was a priority for us too. We had first one, and then two, ping pong tables in the office. Eventually, we moved the ping pong table to one of our two conference rooms to keep the balls from hitting account managers while they were on the phone with clients, and to contain the smell—ping pong is a surprisingly sweaty activity.

We fashioned our monthly agency meetings like radio remote broadcasts, complete with snacks and prizes. They felt like game shows, thanks to our director of operations, Sheri, whose previous career was DJing at a badass rock station. The initial goal of these meetings was thought leadership, communication, and celebration, but it morphed into something else over time. We said hello and goodbye to employees. We celebrated their birthdays, their babies, and their vacations (until we noticed that it was the same person who went on vacation every weekend, and the rest of us hated her for that).

We were a dog-friendly workplace. It started with my very old dog, Boo, who would lie in her bed in the corner of the office, until she started to pace, which meant she needed to go outside for a minute. Boo was an easy dog.

Next was a white Golden Retriever puppy our art director raised in a crate in the office. The dog was sweet, but she would pee on our top client's feet every time she would come into the office. The client would bend over and address Sydney in a high-pitched voice that Sydney loved. She just couldn't contain herself, and there she'd go.

Before too long, we had nine dogs in the office. One dog is one thing. Nine is a whole other business.

We had a photoshoot for the dogs when we redesigned our agency website. The subnavigation in the team section read Creatives, Accounts, Media, Bitches (they were all girl dogs at the time).

Soon, the dogs became an agenda item at our leadership team meetings. We considered a doggy sign-up sheet. We had a dog whisperer come into the office one day to help our dogs get along better. Within months, the office smelled like both a gym, from the ping pong tournaments, and an animal shelter, from the herd. It cost $900 every time we had the carpet cleaned.

This went on for longer than it should have—years—until Hoosier brought the inanity of the situation into specific relief. Hoosier was a Bloodhound who came to work as a puppy and left the size of a Volkswagen. His owner eventually had to chain him to her desk with a 200-pound chain and a cement block.

Dogs bring a cool vibe to an office, and it's shown that they lower blood pressure and increase the sense of happiness the team feels. It's convenient to bring your dog to the office for the day when it has a chiropractor appointment at noon (yes, we had one of those), but this had gotten out of hand. I worried there would be a full-on revolt if I banned the dogs until the day I saw Tom spray Hoosier in the face with a water bottle and mutter, "You f*!%ing stink!" In that moment, I realized that not everybody loved the dogs, and those people mattered too.

My Ambien-induced email to the staff that night went something like this:

"Hey folks, here's the thing…no more dogs in the office."

And that was that.

A STRENGTH TAKEN TOO FAR
BECOMES A WEAKNESS

All of this enthusiasm, fun, and passion did produce good work. The industry was so new that for years, we sold services that we'd never actually done before. That's the type of work that energizes a young, learning team. There's a real freedom in testing with little expectation. When there is no history, everything seems like a success.

Most of the people I hired were new college graduates, about twenty-two years old and looking for their first real job. Digital companies are full of young people for a reason: they grew up with technology, so their understanding is more intuitive, their expectations higher. Their thinking is not confined to the way things have always been, so they are wired to think about how things can be. Young people, with their boundless energy, are fun to have on your team.

In her study, *The Millennial Mandate and the Future of Work: Strategies for Success*, Adrienne Corn, PhD, writes that millennials are the most educated generation in history. They value education and learning. They also value inclusiveness, collaboration, and community. They are interested in personal development and have a growth mindset.[1]

What they don't have is experience. We were a team that people wanted to work with and for, but as digital became a more important part of our clients' businesses and their budgets increased, we began to face internal challenges. A young staff can't understand the pace at which large companies move, or how hard it is for them to try something new. Long planning periods seem like a waste of time. Boards of directors seem extraneous, internal politics like something you could gloss over.

They also don't understand the importance of large clients to a small agency. The consequences of a failed project, an unsettled client, or the loss of a major piece of business mean nothing to them. They are cavalier about client churn, because they are always ready to move on to the next thing, assuming the next client will just walk in the door, ready to sign a contract.

We had a cell phone client for several years, starting with a basic brochure website: heavy on the brand, light on functionality. The cell phone industry is competitive, so through the years that we worked with them, their needs became more and more complex. The iPhone pushed them to another level, bringing high-demand and time-sensitive promotions to the table—which, translated, means nights, weekends, and insane turnaround times for their agencies. We were ecstatic when their strategic plans included a full e-commerce site that would match devices with plans and enable online payment and billing. We were ecstatic, that is, until our brilliant young engineering director moved to the West Coast just after the project kicked off.

From then on, it was a slow death march to the sea. By the time we resigned them, team members were calling in sick on days they knew they were assigned to work on this client. Their needs had quite simply outstripped our capabilities. Our young team was hesitant to admit it, and I was downright resistant. In the end, resignation was inevitable.

Keeping clients is the key to success for a small creative services firm; you rarely get to the good projects in the first year. It takes time to get to know each other and create work that is exciting, effective, and profitable. A long-term relationship is the only way for that to happen, but that notion is anathema to a digital shop full of millennials.

Millennials crave new experiences, so digging deep to support a project that is aging or has gone a little sideways becomes a struggle. Building a predictable, recurring revenue stream isn't interesting, because predictable, recurring business means you're doing maintenance work, and that's boring.

As our clients matured, our greatest strength, the youth of our staff, became our weakness.

WHAT DO WE DO WITH A PROBLEM LIKE MILLENNIALS?

Try to manage a millennial's performance. I dare you. I started Paramore in 2002, just as millennials on the outer bands were finishing college and entering the workforce. In the fifteen years I owned Paramore, every stage of the millennial generation came through the company, and I saw their impact on the business. Much of it was positive, which is encouraging, since they are the future. But a lot of it is unrealistic, and all of it is focused on them. They are known as the "Me Me" generation.

During their interview, the Me Me will hand you a list of vacation days for the next eighteen months, starting the week after their first day on the job.

The Me Me will walk into your office after about six months on the job and ask for a 30 percent raise. The first time this happened I laughed out loud. He didn't.

The Me Me will stare blankly at you when you give them a 20 percent raise with their promotion, and then they will say, "I want 40 percent."

After consulting with his mother, the Me Me will write you a thank-you note for the 40 percent raise, professing loyalty and commitment to the company and laying out the plans for improving his department. Or she will come into your office with a reverent yoga bow, genuinely thankful for the opportunity. Three weeks later, she will bow her way out of the office, leaving her two-week notice behind.

During the two-week notice conversation, the Me Me will want to share their excitement about their new gig with you and the rest of your team. Then they will want a going-away party.

This happened so often that I refused to take the meetings. I stopped showing up on Mondays because that's when they would quit. The promotion, thank you, resignation cycle became so predictable, I'd pitch their thank-you notes in the trash and start the countdown.

I started fantasizing about not coming into the office for the entire month of January. During the lavish Christmas party at my house each year, I'd hand out healthy bonus checks to each employee with a personal note sharing appreciation for all they had done. Then we'd all go have a great Christmas.

In January, they'd start quitting.

Turnover became a serious problem around 2010. Some left for lifestyle reasons or great positions with other companies. Some left because they didn't want to do the work; others just used us to get a job they wanted. There were people who left for Apple, Salesforce, Lonely Planet. There was that asshole who moved to the city and gave me spiritual advice as a parting gift. The first SEO wizard we hired left after ninety days, two weeks after returning from two SEO conferences we paid for him to attend. And our superstar fell in love and moved to the West Coast after I furnished his apartment...in Nashville.

The pattern became predictable particularly with developers. You're most likely to lose them after they've finished the best project they've ever worked on, which is usually less than a year after you've hired them and paid them the most money they've ever made.

You've actually already lost them by the time they request that 30 percent raise. If you don't give it to them, they'll leave right away, and if you do, they'll leave in six weeks. They're not even negotiating with you when they ask for the raise; they're driving up the offer they're negotiating with somebody else. When they accept the other position six weeks later, their starting salary will be $20K higher than the original offer, thanks to you.

My very favorite was when people left to go out on their own and try their hand at freelancing. Because turnover mid-stream is so bad for the project, sometimes we were forced to hire that newly former employee as a freelancer to finish the project—and pay three times what we paid them as a full-time employee. This is a career strategy: get the job, gain trust on the first project, quit during the middle of your second project, get the freelance gig, start your own thing.

Turnover is hard on everyone, particularly during the notice period. Sometimes an employee will offer a longer notice period thinking it will ease the transition. That offer comes with the promise that they will finish their projects, leave them in a good place, and have great transition meetings with the new team.

Instead, what happens is this: they'll do shoddy work while you pay them to prep for their new gig. Every relationship they have in the company will be tarnished as their almost former team members panic at the mountain of work and rework they'll have to do because their friend spent the last two months at the company looking for another job. Then they'll begin to look too—quitting is contagious, just like divorce. As a parting gift, they'll spend their evenings downloading confidential files from your server. Take my advice: decline their long notice period.

Turnover is a serious issue, which is compounded by three intractable problems.

FIRST, A SMALL BUSINESS CAN'T COMPETE WITH THE SALARIES THAT LARGE CORPORATIONS OFFER.

We make up for that in culture, access to clients, and the chance to lead projects. But millennials are impatient with career progression. As soon as they finish their first project, they go for the money and the promotion without the depth of professionalism and experience required to navigate big problems. They often have an overblown sense of the value they bring to your company, wanting to skip from mountaintop to mountaintop without walking through the valley. The pressure to retain talent is high, but here's the truth: when they ask for unreasonable raises, you can't afford to keep them, even though HR says it costs two to four times their salary to replace them. You simply cannot sustain a business when your most expensive full-time talent expects raises of that magnitude. Millennials—in particular web developers and engineers—are pricing themselves out of small businesses.

SECOND, IT'S IMPOSSIBLE TO MANAGE MILLENNIALS' PERFORMANCE WHEN THE INDUSTRY ENCOURAGES THEM TO JOB HOP.

To illustrate this challenge, let's talk developers for a minute, because they hold the key. They are the top-of-the-food-chain workers, not because they are great at their jobs but because there are not enough of them. Traditional colleges and universities are not turning out developers with the knowledge and skills our companies need. Even technical colleges struggle to create a curriculum that is relevant to this ever-changing marketplace. The software schools popping up across the country promise new graduates of their six-month program a job that pays a wage someone six years in the business isn't making. And those new graduates come to you raw, with no project experience and no idea how to be an effective team member.

Developers have the power to make or break a project, speed up or slow down a production schedule. They work with no attachment to the project budget, timeline, or scope of work. Even the most experienced are completely unaccountable to every discipline that makes a company profitable. If they say it doesn't work, it doesn't work. If somebody else built it, it doesn't work. If what they built doesn't work, they blame it on somebody else. If you hold them accountable for their performance, they leave.

And they can, because every company needs them now.

Google this: "Should a web developer job hop," tally the many search results (many of them in favor of job hopping), and then think about trying to build a business around this workforce.

Even the millennials who are not developers are challenging. They are early in their careers, building their resume, refining their skills, and learning what they do and don't want. All of that is understandable and acceptable when you only have a few on your team. When that describes 95 percent of your staff, you've got a big problem.

THIRD, MILLENNIALS ARE NOT MOTIVATED BY LONG-TERM BENEFITS.

Studies show that 60 percent of millennials are open to other job offerings, and 44 percent of them expect to leave their position within six months.[1] In this reality, traditional benefits that reward employees for years of service such as 401Ks and employee stock ownership plans (ESOPs) are worthless. Millennials won't be around long enough to see any of that benefit. Golden handcuffs are extinct for this generation.

At Paramore, we tried every strategy to increase loyalty and retain our talent: parties, acknowledgement, responsibility, a learning culture, a voice in decisions, transparency, big bonuses at the end of the year. Some of it worked. Most of it worked for a minute, and then it became an expectation. As the years went by, I began to resent the expectation that they were due more than their salary, a safe and open workplace, respect, and fun, honest work. They expected more, and more was never enough.

> IN THE BEGINNING OF YOUR BUSINESS, YOU HIRE BECAUSE YOU SEE SO MUCH OPPORTUNITY.

In the beginning of your business, you hire because you see so much opportunity. Eventually, you hire out of pain. Each person you add changes the dynamics of the team, threatening the careful balance of skills and egos, of workloads and talent. As the boss, you approach each new employee with optimism that they will do great things for the company, that they will make a difference. Many of them do, but when they leave, they chip away at your willingness to trust the next one. Studies show that 20 percent of your workforce is in flux at any given time. Gallup estimates that the average millennial disengagement is 55 percent, with another 16 percent who are actively disengaged (meaning they undermine productivity). This leaves only 29 percent of millennials who are engaged at work.[1]

The disengaged employee is death to your company. It's bad when people quit and leave the company. It's worse when they quit and stay.

For many years, our turnover was a fraction of the industry average. But as we matured, and millennials became 95 percent of our workforce, it hit the company—and me personally—so hard that I stopped trying to learn their names. I would look at new employees and assign them a number—the number of months I expected them to stay.

I've been asked if millennials are materially different than any of the previous generations. Did baby boomers feel the same way about Gen X? Did the Greatest Generation feel this way about the Silent Generation? It is true that we always feel that the younger generation doesn't work as hard as we did, that they have more advantages than we had. But I believe we are seeing something completely different that will have far-reaching impact on business in our country. This is the first generation to have access to the same movies, fashions, and music as others across the country and across the globe. The internet allows us to share every thought immediately, to be friends with people everywhere, to experience different cultures and blend them into our daily lives. As one millennial said to me, "We're all just picking up cues from each other."

This is not an absolutely new phenomenon. Teacher resource and professional development website Annenberg Learner says, in their multimedia course on global pop culture, that, "The diffusion of popular culture across frontiers and boundaries has been taking place for millennia. Music, games, and jokes traveled with the caravans along the Silk Road, accompanied the armies of the Crusades, and sailed across the oceans in ships during the age of exploration. However, the globalization of popular culture during the twentieth century was more extensive, more pervasive, and more penetrating than during previous eras.[2]"

That rapid globalization of pop culture is affecting our companies. Dr. Corn, author of *The Millennial Mandate and the Future of Work,* says that millennials are the first global generation to share generational characteristics and approach work differently than older generations of workers. They will disrupt organizational culture to accommodate their values and views of work and life.

This might be beneficial in the long run, but it is all painful in the beginning.

That disruption is happening right now. By 2025, millennials will be 75 percent of the workforce.

At Paramore, constant turnover put us in jeopardy of

project failures, which is one of a dozen reasons to lie awake at night. It eroded confidence across the company. Business Development, the lifeblood of an agency, was afraid to sell because it became so hard to complete projects. Account Services and Media lost their faith in the Production department after seeing the clients' disappointment over and over.

Small agencies are lean, agile, and smart, but they do not have a deep bench. When turnover becomes a problem, your entire business is at risk. Clients hire you for your experience and expertise, which walks out the door at the end of a two-week notice. At that point, you are left to deliver what the client hired you to deliver without the people and skills that helped you win the business.

When your expertise walks out the door, are you still an expert? No. You are simply left to rebuild your team, over and over.

YOU ARE LEFT TO REBUILD YOUR TEAM

We work in a deadline-driven world. Nothing gets done until it absolutely can't go on without being done anymore, and so it was with building a leadership team at Paramore. When it finally hurt so much that I couldn't put it off any longer, I got serious about it. This seemed to be the answer to more than one issue. After several years in business, I had some superstars who both needed and wanted more responsibility and authority. We needed to stabilize our team, to hire more qualified people, keep them longer, and minimize the drama. I personally was stretched to the max with the load of leading the company and being the face of the company too. I was becoming deaf to the demands of the team.

As we reached what turned out to be the midpoint of the business with me as owner and CEO, I worked on this transition with my strategy coach, Liz Allen Fey. In one session, she asked me what my job was. By this time, I was no longer the expert in digital, so I couldn't do the client work myself like I did for the first few years. My job had changed. I was running the business, focusing outwardly to build the brand, and finding opportunities to grow. The team was doing the client work.

We wrote my job description in about a minute, using five bullet points on a note card:

- Grow and mentor the leadership team
- Set vision and direction for the company
- Be the face of the company
- Manage the finances
- Be available for key relationships

I read that note card every day. It became the foundation for the next stage of growth at Paramore. Once I understood who I was and where I fit into the company, we finally had a model for the rest of the staff.

We organized the company under four VPs: Operations, Sales, Accounts, and Production. I did what most accidental business owners do: promoted the hardest working people to lead the departments and filled in the gaps myself.

Nurturing talent from within became the Paramore way. It created excitement and loyalty, two things that make a business owner feel good. This structure gave us clarity and helped us reach our highest revenue years. We created our most meaningful work during that time as well, but the side effects were troubling.

I hated the divisions I was seeing between departments. Actually, I hated having departments at all. As we hovered between eighteen to twenty-five employees, factions developed, and we entered periods of high drama. Drama is not all bad, mind you; people do their best work when they are emotionally bought-in, but emotions come with a price.

There were regular conflicts between the creative director and the accounts people, and between accounts and business development. We would work hard as a team to win a new client, but before the ink was dry, the same team would throw up one objection after another to the actual work. At first blush, it looked like these conflicts were altruistic in nature. The directors would quote the company's core values to me in defense of their position. I would get drawn in to settle disputes. There were tears. But we were young and growing; surely this was normal.

This industry is competitive, and new business is very difficult to win. Good clients with a successful product and a healthy budget to match are not waiting right outside your door, but your staff doesn't understand that. For them, work does just show up on their desk with a deadline. They have no skin in the game. While you want your team to be engaged, you alone are financially responsible for the business.

We had our first mutiny over a client when every man on our creative team refused to work on *Maxim*. I hate pornography in every form, but let's be honest, there's not much difference between *Maxim* and any number of other magazines featuring beautiful, scantily clad women on the cover. In Nashville, there are only so many international brands, so it was tough for me to step away from this one.

So I fought. I rationalized. I sought advice and wrestled with myself every night, until one of the guys came to me and said, "You have a company that people tie to their moral values. You can't ask for more dedication than that."

I declined the business, but it was the first time I was truly angry with the team. More than missing out on the potential revenue, what angered me was the team's assumption that they could dictate which clients we took. That is a slippery slope.

I looked at the staff differently after that confrontation and began to notice something else: the arguments sounded less altruistic and more focused on their own portfolios. The team was passive aggressively controlling the client base— slowing down on projects they hated, doing marginal work for clients they didn't relate to, inflating estimates when they didn't want the work. Trying to manage creative millennials is like trying to push a string uphill: it can't be done.

Developing a leadership team was a good first step, but it came with its own challenges. At first, it feels good to have a leadership team who's eager to learn and take responsibility. They bring valuable ideas to the company. They relieve you of the daily stress of managing a huge team. As my good friend and mentor John Sharpe says, managing a large team on your own is like being nibbled to death by a duck. It doesn't hurt too badly at first but eventually it leads to a long, painful death.

In building the leadership team, we went through true alignment of responsibility, authority, and financial reward for each person. We communicated it to the company, and we took off like a rocket ship. The plan worked. Things became more sane.

And then life happened.

On the senior leadership team, we had two millennials, two Gen X's and two baby boomers, including me. When our Gen X VP of Sales fell in love with a golfer, had a baby, and moved to St. Simon's, where her husband lived, I knew our company would hurt. At the time, not having fallen in love with my own golf pro yet, I couldn't understand her rationale.

"You'd move to an island with a golfer?!" I'd exclaimed.

"I don't understand it either," she replied tearfully. "But I have to get my family in the same state."

We had babies and drug abuse, divorces and domestic violence. We had a new employee who just couldn't make it into the office because she was trying to heal her dogs' urinary tract infections herself. We had big wins and big losses. We had equal parts fun and pain.

It is an honor to build leaders. It's gratifying to see them grow and to see the impact they have on their teams. Others are inspired by their success and step up to carve out their own opportunities. We built leaders, and the company grew with them.

The goodness of building leaders goes far beyond your own company. In the United States, 93 percent of companies are small businesses. The real gift small business gives to the world is the development of young talent into gifted leaders who go out into the world to do great things and, ultimately, repeat the cycle by nurturing other leaders.

But their going out into the world is what hurts you so much.

After the initial excitement at being named VP and the success of the first couple of years under this new structure, the young leaders began to struggle with the realities of their responsibilities. They each eventually ran out of steam from a combination of personal trauma and just plain fatigue. It is hard to manage your friends. Division between departments was deeper than ever. There were problems that we just couldn't seem to solve. Managing the constant churn and change in the industry, along with the employees while they were building families and maturing as people, is tough stuff.

The truth about a team is that you don't just build it once. You have to keep building it day after day, adjusting not only your needs and expectations but theirs as well. As your expertise is walking out the door to other opportunities, your leadership team is left to deal with the gap their departure creates. As their leader, you lean heavily on your ability to inspire confidence, fearlessly facing each clue that someone is drifting, or even the best relationships will sour.

THE TRUTH ABOUT A TEAM IS THAT YOU DON'T JUST BUILD IT ONCE.

During one of the most stressful times dealing with employee and client churn, my most steady, dependable VP said to me, "It's a zero-sum game. At the end of the day, you have paid me for the work I have done, and we are even."

I didn't respond at the time because I had to let that one sit in my head for a bit. It took me two years to understand why he was wrong.

Senior leaders are not hourly workers. Their compensation; level of autonomy, authority, and influence; and access to intellectual property and confidential information about the business changes the game. When they are young and promoted into a senior position, the value they add is far less than their cost to the business. You aren't paying them for the work they are doing right now. You're investing in them for the work they will do for years to come.

After several successful but stressful years with a young leadership team, we entered a time of big transition. Within a year, I lost them all for reasons ranging from love to burglary. The thought of rebuilding that core team was almost more than I could bear. I did not know if I could do it again. It takes time to heal and jumping right in with other people didn't feel right.

The commitment you make to one another is similar to a marriage, so when they leave, it is like getting a divorce. (I should know. I've had three of them.)

By this time, leadership meetings had grown to include almost a third of the company, way too many for the level of transparency required to solve problems. Young leaders aren't ready for the truth about small business. The meetings became a drama-filled hour or two of posturing and tears where issues got worse, not better. Personal agendas clouded the judgement of my young VPs, and I lost the will to bring them back around.

On my walk home from work one beautiful evening during this time, I had an epiphany. It was so clear that I stopped walking and stood on the sidewalk at Church Street Park, processing this thought: "I'll never hire anyone my age again."

I felt extremely sad.

During the two years prior, I had thought seriously about the next stage of the business. You're supposed to have a succession plan, but I did not have one. What would I do with what I had built? Questions like this will not let you go until you have settled them, and you can't settle them until you find a truth-teller. Mine was my lawyer, Tommy Estes.

"Why do you want to do anything at all?" Tommy asked when he came to my office to discuss succession planning.

"So that if I die, the business will be able to continue," I replied. "The employees will have jobs and the clients will be taken care of."

Tommy said, "Why? You're dead."

I said, "Tell me more about that."

"Hannah, you have a nice business, but respectfully, it's not a huge legacy to leave the city," he explained, almost echoing my client from years earlier. "It's not Ingram Industries or The Frist Foundation. What you really want is to take care of your family."

"We're good there."

"Well, you might have a non-profit you want to benefit," Tommy said. "But in either case, your employees will find another job within days, and your clients will find another agency faster than that. You need to think about what you want to do for yourself and for the ones you love."

Then Tommy closed with the right question: "Is what you want really a succession plan, or is it a retention plan?"

I wanted a retention plan so I wouldn't be left alone, holding the bag.

And boy, did I try to create one. I appointed the two oldest people besides me to VP status, even though they lived in other states, just to retain some more seasoned experience—and to ease the pain of being the only old person in the company. I almost mortgaged all of my property to provide golden handcuffs for my entire eight-person leadership team. In the end, remote VPs did not work out, and my financial advisors looked at me sideways over the retention plan. Common sense prevailed.

Since the seventh year in business, I had become obsessed with the fear that I would miss a major pivot in the business or the industry, and that my oversight would take us down. In retrospect, that's exactly what happened.

At a critical point in the business, when I needed to bring in senior-level expertise to solve problems and get us ready for the next stage of growth, I missed the pivot. I promoted from within instead of going outside to bring in the talent we needed.

And with good reason; growing a leadership team is the biggest relationship risk a business owner takes. You have to show them all the vulnerable parts of the business— how frequently you are close to going out of business, how much money each bad decision costs, how many mistakes you make, your own insecurities—knowing that it might scare them so much that they leave. But there is no other way to do it.

GROWING A LEADERSHIP TEAM IS THE BIGGEST RELATIONSHIP RISK A BUSINESS OWNER TAKES.

As the owner of a business that's dependent on young talent, you face the fact that you only have them for a small space of time. Time marches on and so do they, leaving you to hold the bag.

YOU'RE EXACTLY WHERE YOU ARE SUPPOSED TO BE

I often start to work things out on paper when I am puzzling through a problem. Sometimes I stand in front of a white board and just write down simple things; thoughts, lists, ramblings. Through the years, as I was learning to build a leadership team and the company was experiencing double- and triple-digit growth every year, things were hard for me at home. It turns out, you just can't be great everywhere at the same time. I was grieving my own children who were spreading their wings. I was divorcing, again, and wondering what life would be like, being single in my 50s, when a very clear thought took root in my mind:

You are exactly where you are supposed to be.

The thought continued, *Your children will always be your children and you will always love them, but they aren't the only people who need you. Look outside your door.*

And so I did. Right outside my office door were twenty or so young people, most of them diligently trying to contribute to the company's success. Sharing a space of time with them and watching them grow, fail, and, yes, even leave, became a sacred time in my life.

I looked at them differently, loving the diversity and the passion they brought—along with the drama that you just can't separate from the package—and we raced to the top of our game during the years that followed.

Through the years, as that feeling moved from being sacred to being scary, from the threat of failure and the fear of being left alone with a failed business, I had yet another epiphany:

When you're forty-two and hiring twenty-two-year-olds, that's one thing. When you're fifty-seven and still hiring twenty-two-year-olds, it's a whole other thing. The gap was too large to span. I no longer related to my team in the same way. I didn't even understand them—and worse, I didn't want to. I didn't care about their dogs and their destination weddings. I resented their illusion of work/life balance, which leaves their employer teetering. It was no longer fun for me to work through the challenges of raw talent in an emerging industry. I craved the fellowship of peers.

At that time, Paramore was full of about thirty talented, mostly awesome people. People who made me angry every day.

It was time for me to go.

---

1 Outsell: The Millennial Mandate and the Future of Work: Strategies For Success by Adrienne Corn, PhD

2 Annenberg Learner, Unit 25: https://www.learner.org/courses/worldhistory/unit_main_25.html

KEY TAKEAWAYS

1. **A young staff in an emerging industry is prone to turnover.**
   - Study your industry to determine the level of risk you are carrying regarding turnover.
   - Network with other owners in your space to create support in your market and mitigate the impact of employees hopping from one company to the other, driving up salary costs along the way.

2. **Young leaders aren't mature enough to handle large clients and company growth.**
   - Recruit specifically for the leadership team.
   - Hire more senior people for VP slots rather than promoting twenty-somethings because you don't want to lose them.
   - Get input from inside and outside your industry on appropriate compensation and bonus levels. Being too generous in the early days won't be sustainable as you grow.

3. **Feeling alone at the top.**
   - Search for your number two by the time you are in your fifth year.
   - This person must want to be the CEO eventually and needs to be more senior with direct experience.

4. **Build culture intentionally with an eye toward sustainability.**
   - Find the right mix for your company and think forward ten years down the road when you have three times the number of employees. Culture gets expensive and unsustainable if you go too big in the beginning.

5. Learn the right amount of transparency for your company.

- Don't over-share about your personal life, especially if it affects work-life balance and culture.
- Protect confidential information rigorously. Nobody keeps secrets.

— CHAPTER THREE —

THE CLIENTS
MANAGING DISAPPOINTMENT

"You start losing a client the day you sign them," John Sharpe said to me one day.

I looked at him quizzically and tried to dismiss his remark. I didn't understand this defeatist comment coming from my mentor. I'd met John just before starting my business, and from the first day, I'd trusted everything he said. He is full of wisdom and experience, and he is always right—unfortunately so in this case—but I didn't buy it at the time. We were in a very new, developing industry, and my company, Paramore Digital, was winning all the time. Our team expanded as our revenue grew, and our work was good. There was more opportunity than we could handle, but we never said no. We grew with each client we won, and I thought John was wrong.

Closing business was easy at first. We were ahead of

the curve, before the game-changing year of 2007. Before the iPhone was invented, before Facebook was available to everyone, before Twitter, before the cloud, before most companies had their customer's email addresses. Because of this, we got to plow some fun ground. Our relationships were good, and so were our results. For years, every time I sold something, we'd never actually provided that service before. We were the first agency to run any kind of digital campaign— email, PPC, lead generation, display, etc.— for most of the clients we had during our first seven years in business. My growth projections were off the charts, because I thought good results and good relationships were enough to keep clients.

They weren't. They aren't.

In 2002, digital agencies were a new thing. We were the hipper counterpart to the older style, traditional advertising agency. We were more approachable. We had fewer processes and no procedures. We had more toys in our office. We wore ripped jeans and t-shirts. Clients were attracted to us, and the feeling was mutual, but we were not needy. We were a no-strings relationship.

Since the beginning, ad agencies had been built on long-term relationships with their clients, locked down through strong contracts and Jack Daniels. Many agencies were started when large companies dispatched marketing veterans from their ranks, promising their business as the foundational client for their new agency. Agency principals sacrificed their livers to their clients in exchange for commitments like that, and it worked. It was successful for decades, enabling many of today's largest brands to become today's largest brands. But over time, contracts tended to protect turf rather than provide a space for creativity and innovation. For a variety of reasons, the work got stuck.

The traditional agency/client relationship had been under attack for a while by the time we started Paramore Digital. *Ad Age* and other industry publications began writing about this issue at the turn of the century, and the more prominent digital became, the worse the problem got. Agencies grew more protective of their relationships and tried with all their might to slot digital into a box, just like print, radio, and TV. But a seismic shift was taking place across the globe, spurred on by the rapid changes in technology that aged out many of the skill sets that had been the basis of the agency/client relationship.

In other words, technology changed everything. Production budgets fell when video cameras got cheap and the editing software that once took up a whole room was now available on a laptop. Clients no longer had the patience for long-term return on ad spending when Google Adwords showed results in minutes. The model of real strategic thinking with a long-term partner began to decrease as technology increased.

The shorter-term results digital enabled were attractive to clients, and their traditional agency relationship began to feel like a loveless marriage with a partner who used to be beautiful.

And here we came with our ripped jeans.

We won so consistently and grew so fast for the first seven years that I didn't see an end to it. Not knowing anything about the agency model or this dysfunction when I started Paramore Digital, John's statement didn't make any sense to me. But it haunted me.

THE FIRST LOSS

We got our first million-dollar account in the second year of business, when paid search was so new, we didn't know what to call it. Our first budget with this durable medical equipment company, which sold direct to consumer through a Medicare loophole, was $5,000. The budget lasted about four days. For years, all of their leads had come from TV and direct mail, but as digital grew, those numbers declined. When we opened the spigot on Google, it created a new gushing lead flow with all the potential of hyper targeting, tracking, and flexibility.

I personally lived and breathed this campaign of hundreds of words and phrases. I'd built it from scratch, and we were selling literally millions of dollars of product for them. Quickly, we were in the grind of higher and higher expectations every day, and as our numbers climbed, their wallets opened wider. Within a few weeks, their monthly budget with us was $125,000, and we were seriously in the digital media business.

They called us partners and threw money our way after short, urgent phone calls that always began with, "If you had $10,000 more tomorrow, how many more leads could you get?"

And that was their strategy: more money, more leads. Today.

On our end, the strategy was to do whatever it took to keep that money coming in. Check on the campaign throughout the night? Okay. Check again with my coffee in the morning? Um hum. Check while on vacation? Yes. Of course.

Partner attitude was what we had. Vendor was what we were to them, replaced in an instant with an upstart who came in through the back door, the same way we'd entered. No explanation.

Although they were our largest client, their loss wasn't hard to recover from. We were still very young, and I thought they were a one-off. They were not normal and appreciative like real clients would be. We tested and learned so many things on that client that we just continued going with an imperceptible effect on the bottom line after they were gone. Unfortunately, they would not be the last large client we would lose after a wildly successful ride.

REPEAT IN PARADISE

Tourism was one of the industries to benefit quickly from digital. Like healthcare and education, vacations are big purchases. They are rare for most people, so a lot of thought and research goes into planning a vacation. Even though Paramore Digital was located in Nashville, the mecca of healthcare, we decided early on that we preferred hotel beds over hospital beds so away we went, carving out a specialty in tourism marketing.

It was a great experience. For years, we worked with tourism organizations and destinations across the country. We had hotels and resorts, including The Greenbrier in White Sulphur Springs, West Virginia, and La Torretta Del Lago outside of Houston. We had attractions like Morey's Piers in Wildwood, New Jersey, and Adventures on the Gorge in West Virginia. We had well-known destinations such as Gatlinburg, Tennessee, and Polk County, Florida. For twelve years, we traveled and pitched and experienced the destinations. It was so much fun.

The budgets were modest at first, but within a handful of years, several of them approached the $1 million mark, and we were creating the best work of the agency's life. The lines had begun to blur between traditional and digital marketing as we matured, and our clients aged, and our work began to cross over.

Which is where the going got tough. There is danger in the crossover. Ask any musician.

For a long time, we were the digital agency of record for a state tourism department. They became a foundational client for us, the largest and the most influential we would ever have. With budgets big enough to get noticed, the work we did for them opened doors for us in tourism around the country.

In 2012, after seven years of working with this client,

their state entered a very political time for the industry. With a new oversight board put in place by the governor to monitor the work of the tourism department's staff, the state tripled the tourism budget and developed an appetite for an international agency. Initially, our digital contract was not supposed to be a part of the request for proposal (RFP), but in the end we were, swept up in a boardroom debate in the rush of politically motivated decisions. Our only option was to go for broke—all or nothing.

We got nothing. The crossover had failed. The day after we moved into a brand-new office downtown, we got the call that our relationship was over.

One year later, the same thing happened with the client that was at that time our largest. In yet another power-motivated move by the board of directors, and after five years of record-breaking work, we pitched to retain our current contract and expand the scope to include all traditional and digital marketing (after again being told our current contract was not in jeopardy). At the end of our pitch to this group of thirty board members, they stood up and applauded, and the chairman of the board said, "You are the model we hold up for all of your competitors. We had nothing when you started working with us five years ago. What you have done is tremendous. You are trustworthy and present. You are family."

I broke into a cold sweat. I knew immediately that we were screwed, because that's what family does; they screw you.

John's words from fourteen years earlier came back to

me, "You start losing a client the day you sign them."

Over fifteen years, we won business and lost business in an almost nonsensical manner. What makes people decide one thing or another is a mystery. Sometimes we deserved to lose the client, but I noticed something over time; we never lost a major piece of business because we had done bad work. We always lost big clients because of something outside our control, such as a mandated RFP, a shift in the industry, a change in the leadership at the company, or a power struggle on the board. It's hard not to be offended when a client says your work was the most effective work ever done for them in the letter they write you to inform you they're replacing you with someone else.

Big clients get the attention of the whole agency, and they are game-changers. But there is a flip side. Big clients suck up agency resources to the detriment of creativity and other clients. There are a number of disconnects between what they need and what they buy. They don't actually like the model of an agency; while they want the agency's expertise, they rarely trust it, and they don't like paying for it. Occasionally, their leaving is a blessing. But usually it hurts. It means layoffs, because the next big client is not waiting outside your door for space to open up at your firm; they're still busy abusing another agency.

THE PROBLEM WITH CLIENTS

Those experiences and others like them were painful but not out of the norm, as it turns out. The American Association of Advertising Agencies reports that the average tenure of an agency/client relationship has gone from more than six years to less than thirty-three months. Another related study shows that the average tenure of a chief marketing officer (CMO) on the brand side is forty-four months.

Think about that for a minute. Thirty-three months from start to finish, with a new CMO, in a disruptive industry. How much good work can you do in a situation like that?

Almost none. There isn't enough time.

The agency model is broken. I wish it wasn't true, but I believe it is. There are too many disconnects between the model of a successful agency and the client's expectations for it to work anymore. Some of these disconnects have been developing for decades. Others are a result of the digital disruption, which put sophisticated technology into everyone's hands and devalued the work. Either way, the model no longer works because what a client wants from an agency and what the agency needs to survive are too far apart.

There are seven main disconnects that I've found to be standing in the way of successful client/agency rapport, and great long-lasting work.

DISCONNECT #1:
PROJECTS VERSUS RELATIONSHIPS

The agency of record (AOR) relationship is a thing of the past. Clients are more likely to have a handful of agencies who offer overlapping services rather than to trust one agency with all of their work. Instead of committing to a full relationship with an agency or a technology partner, they hire you for projects.

Sometimes that's the right thing to do, because nobody is an expert at everything now, but mid-sized firms trying to live project to project spells almost certain death. Having multiple agencies at the table, all vying for a larger share of a pie that is already too small, is a bad situation. Nobody is paid enough to really care about your business. Instead of working for the long-term good of the clients, agencies are working to keep the lights on.

DISCONNECT #2:
TIME AND MONEY

Let's face it: the only thing an agency has to charge you for is time. I can hear folks shouting now: "We should be charging for ideas and expertise!" That'd be great, but there's no real way to do that for most firms; it's too nebulous an idea to build a business on. Our hourly rate reflects the quality of our ideas and the depth of our expertise. We charge for time.

And let's face this, too: clients hate to pay for time, and they have no idea how long it takes to do good work, either creatively or technically.

Particularly in digital, the work is undervalued because of the transparency of the web and the reputation that projects are quick and easy. The reality is that when mistakes are made, or a change in strategy dictates reworking part of the project, there are major clashes over who is responsible and the impact it will have on the project's budget and timeline. The agency is often expected to take all project risk, even though the client rarely has the knowledge and experience necessary to competently manage the project on their side.

DISCONNECT #3:
CLIENTS DON'T KNOW WHAT THEY NEED

Another reason that time and money are issues is because the client doesn't know what their business really needs to succeed, which bloats the project and creates flawed expectations. Creative projects are exciting, and because anything is possible, the clients often continue to tack on ideas and expand their expectations until the strategy is secondary to the bells and whistles.

At Paramore Digital, we kicked off every new client relationship with a discovery session. We asked our clients to invite to the meeting all the people who would be key stakeholders in the project—managers who had information we would need, people who would need to approve the project, etc., so we could build consensus during the meeting and come out with a clear scope of work and an accurate budget. Here's what happened...

WE WOULD LEAVE THE MEETING
WITH THIS UNDERSTANDING:

WHAT THE CLIENT SAYS THEY NEED:

WE WOULD GO BACK TO OUR OFFICES
AND WRITE THE SCOPE OF WORK:

WHAT WE HEARD:

WHAT THE CLIENT SAYS THEY NEED:

WE WOULD WORK FOR WEEKS/MONTHS ON THE PROJECT AND END UP HERE:

WHAT WE BUILT:

WHAT WE HEARD:

WHAT THE CLIENT SAYS THEY NEED:

AFTER LAUNCH WE WOULD FIND OUT:

WHAT WE BUILT:

WHAT WE HEARD:

WHAT THE CLIENT SAYS THEY NEED:

WHAT THE CLIENT REALLY NEEDS:

WHEN WE DID OUR FINAL BILLING WE WOULD FIND OUT:

WHAT WE BUILT:

WHAT WE HEARD:

WHAT THE CLIENT SAYS THEY NEED:

WHAT THE CLIENT REALLY NEEDS:

WHAT THE CLIENT'S BUDGET CAN AFFORD: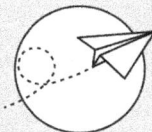

AT THE PROJECT REVIEW MEETING WE WOULD LEARN:

WHAT WE BUILT:

WHERE THE PROFIT WENT

WHAT WE HEARD:

WHERE THE PROFIT WENT

WHAT THE CLIENT SAYS THEY NEED:

WHERE THE PROFIT WENT

WHAT THE CLIENT REALLY NEEDS:

WHERE THE PROFIT WENT

WHAT THE CLIENT'S BUDGET CAN AFFORD:

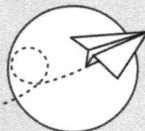

Lessons gleaned from these interactions were that:
1. What the client can afford is less than what they really need.
2. What the client really needs is less than what they tell the agency they need.
3. What the agency hears is more than what the client says they need.
4. What the agency builds is exponentially more than what they heard.

All of the agency's profitability in the project was lost between what the client could really afford and what we built for them.

The end result for the client is a project that is overbuilt and off point.

And the relationship between the agency and the client is strained. We didn't make money, and they didn't get what they really need.

DISCONNECT #4: CLIENTS AREN'T CREATIVE EXPERTS.. BUT THEY THINK THEY ARE.

Henry David Thoreau wrote that "most men live lives of quiet desperation and die with their soul still inside them." Boy, I can tell you that he was predicting the modern-day client.

Most businesspeople live uncreative, boring lives. They are stuck in the land of spreadsheets and board meetings, just dying for somebody to ask them what they think of the wallpaper in the bathroom, or the company's logo, or what they would like to see on their company's website.

If they get a chance to participate in a collaborative creative project, they won't stick to what they should really be doing—bringing their knowledge of the company to the table for the agency to work with. All of a sudden, they are experts at fonts and images and content. They are all marketing experts. Having started a collaborative process, the manager doesn't want to shut them down, so we end up with the worst of all possible scenarios: the Frankenstein design.

In the end, the work is less effective than it should be, and the agency takes the blame.

DISCONNECT #5: AGENCIES CREATE ESTIMATES. CLIENTS HAVE BUDGETS.

In our first eight years, the websites we built were fairly simple. Our clients had not moved to digital in their core business functions, so the websites were pretty much stand-alone pieces, and they only had to work on desktop computers. By the end of my time at Paramore Digital, the websites we built were almost enterprise level, requiring multiple third-party tie-ins with things such as billing systems, booking engines, customer profiles, and more, all built on different platforms, and they all had to work flawlessly across every imaginable device: desktop, phone, tablet, Android, and iOS.

We lost money so many times on those projects that

I became convinced of two things: 1) you can't accurately scope any project that costs more than $75,000, and 2) agile budgeting is the right way to approach custom projects.

The problem is, our clients don't have agile budgets. They want custom development work for a project price because they have fixed budgets. And this is the basic problem: clients have defined budgets, but agencies create price estimates.

> **AND THIS IS THE BASIC PROBLEM: CLIENTS HAVE DEFINED BUDGETS, BUT AGENCIES CREATE PRICE ESTIMATES.**

There is no such thing as an accurate estimate. An estimate is an estimate. It will change as we get further into the project, setting up some of the toughest conversations that agencies have with their clients.

DISCONNECT #6: CLIENTS SAY THEY WANT STRATEGY—BUT THEY DON'T.

Clients are impatient with the strategic process. They'd rather have a whole bunch of transactional wins and retrofit a strategy to it when it's time for a board meeting than to do the real work...because most of them don't know the difference between a strategy and a tactic.

Short-term tactics are like a drug; they provide an instant hit. Strategy is like physical therapy; it's slow-going. Strategy doesn't look like it will accomplish anything, until it finally does. But it doesn't work at all if you don't put strategy first.

DISCONNECT #7: CLIENTS DON'T WANT YOU TO MAKE A PROFIT ON THEIR WORK.

Possibly the largest disconnect in this dysfunctional relationship is that clients want to work with a successful agency, but they don't really want you to make money on their business. They negotiate you down to an hourly rate that you cannot survive on and then refuse to pay for the additional work required when the project grows beyond the original plans.

People are so focused on always getting "a deal" that they forget that agencies are in business to make money, too. This creates a relationship that is out of balance. The agency puts forward their best thinking in order to make the client successful, but the client wants us to work basically at cost. Not only is that an unsustainable situation for the agency, but eventually the client loses, too. They won't get the agency's best work if they aren't willing to pay for it. The relationship devolves. That's particularly true when hurt feelings coming from inside the agency translate into dishonoring the client, something I vowed to never do.

HONOR THE CLIENT

At Paramore Digital, we had nine core values. The most difficult one to put into practice day to day was "Honor the

Client." The rest of that core value said, "We treat the client with respect even when they aren't in the room."

This meant that if you were having a bad day with a client, you weren't allowed to bleed all over the rest of the staff, who might have had only good interactions with the same client. It meant that if there was a conflict, you honored the client enough to address it head-on. It meant that you supported clients in the community and that you fought for their best interest inside the agency.

If we found we couldn't abide by this core value, we did one thing: we resigned the client.

I'd like to be able to say that our clients were the reason we were successful, but that's not always true. They hired us, and most of the time they paid us, but often they didn't pay us enough to support the amount of time and expertise they had consumed. We had to fight to get additional budget when the client would scope creep the project. We had to defend the rework required when the client changed their mind halfway through a project. We had to chase businesses owned by some of the most successful people in Nashville to get them to pay their invoices. It was infuriating.

At the end of the day, the first priority of any business is to stay in business, because we can't please a client, provide jobs, or change the world if we can't stay in business.

THE FIRST PRIORITY OF ANY BUSINESS IS TO STAY IN BUSINESS.

I found I could no longer honor the client when the norm was that they expected more than they paid for, to the point that it was hard to stay in business. It was such a consistent issue that I finally realized this: clients disrespect the business model of their agencies.

Game over.

WHY DOES THIS HURT SO MUCH?

In 2015, I met a bank president named Bill Nigh on a Leadership Study Mission with the Nashville Area Chamber of Commerce. We had the good fortune of having boarding passes one number apart on our Southwest Airlines flight to Salt Lake City, so we sat together. Over the next four hours, I showed him my spreadsheets tracking my progress in golf. I know, it's embarrassing. He acted impressed, because he's a nice guy and he's a golfer too.

Not long after we returned from that trip, I was dealing with some of the toughest issues we would ever have with revenue and profits. After a few conversations over a few months, Bill finally said, "Hannah, why don't you come over here for lunch? Bring your numbers with you. I'll order sandwiches, we'll go through them, and I'll tell you what I see."

I said, "How about tomorrow?"

I headed into the bank president's office with my arms full of binders and my big calculator.

Bill and I went through years of data and my profit and loss (P&L) statements for a good forty-five minutes.

He listened to me whine about clients and employees and change and revenue and profit and on and on. Then he looked at me and said, "You just described every company in America."

Every industry is struggling to find a trained or trainable workforce. Every business has high turnover and increasing competition. They all have peaks and valleys in revenue and profits. They all have ungrateful clients.

He went on to point out all the good things about our numbers and focused on my ability to steer the business and control my destiny. He said, "Do you think that just because I'm the president of this bank that I'm safe in my job? There is no security, and there is no loyalty. I think what you're hurting over is the people side."

Bill was right. Paramore Digital was successful. We had better-than-average everything—clients, staff, culture—and yet we struggled.

> ## THE THING ABOUT CLIENTS IS THAT LOSING THEM IS REALLY HARD, BUT SO IS KEEPING THEM.

The thing about clients is that losing them is really hard, but so is keeping them. I hated the inequity of the relationship, their expectation that they could have the best work for a small price, the passive/aggressiveness of the board, and the constant struggle to keep them happy so that we could get to the good work.

BUSINESS OWNERS COMMIT TO THE ENTIRE INFRASTRUCTURE OF A BUSINESS TO SERVE THE CLIENT, WHO WON'T MAKE A COMMITMENT BACK TO THEM.

And I never got used to the sudden absence of a relationship we'd spent so much time nurturing and growing. For no good reason at all, they would leave, usually all of a sudden. While this is totally normal in business, it is also totally painful. I often felt like the mother of a teenager, stunned and hurting over the way they were treating me after I'd carried them in my womb for nine months, then nurtured and loved and provided for them. I wanted to scream, "Look at what we've done for you!"

People don't leave well.

This is true for all industries, but for the independent business owner, it is magnified. Business owners commit to the entire infrastructure of a business—the office, staff, training, benefits, and more—and take a personal financial risk on the success of the firm in order to serve the client, who won't make a commitment back to them.

After years of this, it got to the point that every client loss sent me into a tailspin. No matter what the norms or trends are, entrepreneurs always fear they are going to lose the business overnight. And it is a slippery slope. Client losses, especially after the work has been good, are hard on the staff. With every major loss, I could see in the team members' eyes that they would not commit as deeply the next time. We all became jaded, knowing that no matter what we did, eventually we would lose clients for no good reason.

This chapter has been hard to write because I loved so many of our clients. Without them, we wouldn't have had fifteen successful years. Their willingness to trust first me and then the Paramore Digital team is something for which I will always be grateful. I appreciated the ones that committed to the relationship and rode through some storms with us. We were better on the other side of those storms. There were several clients like that, but there were not enough.

I don't have the answer for how to fix this. Perhaps agencies will go the way of the VHS tape. And yet companies need access to creative people who can think about their businesses differently.

I know one thing for sure: there's not a magic pill. If there were, I would have taken it.

KEY TAKEAWAYS

The central problem with clients is the disparity between their lack of commitment to the agency and the agency's need to staff for both the highs and the lows of their clients needs. In a services firm, the project flow is almost unpredictable.

1. Project vs. retainer relationships.

- Consistently analyze your business model so that you can staff appropriately. This could be a mix of full-time and contract employees.
- Ruthlessly seek out solutions for the work that can be done by contract employees. Be open to offshoring.

2. Not right-sizing my staff when we lost major clients.

- When you lose a major client, right-size your staff immediately.

3. Be bottom-heavy, not top-heavy.

- Invest in a couple of rock-star managers. Don't let the leadership team balloon to include one-third of the company.
- Flesh out the staff level to relieve pressure there and create elasticity when you have to downsize.

— CHAPTER FOUR —

THE BUSINESS

GROWING UP IS HARD

I had terrible jobs for a long time. My dad was a minister and my mother was a housewife, so my childhood was conservative and focused on church. I'm glad my childhood was shaped by the church, but there was no talk in my family of what we would do to make money when we grew up. And then, when I was seventeen years old, my parents split up. It's not uncommon for that to happen in ministerial families now, but in 1976, it was rare—and taboo. Our family struggled and stumbled and then fell completely apart, right at the time when I should have been thinking about the future. I'd studied piano for a long time, so when it came time for me to make a college decision, absent any other ideas, I enrolled in the music program at Belmont College (now Belmont University).

I didn't last long. Without a foundation, it's easy to crumble.

I got married young and went to work, thinking I'd go back to school in a couple years. But for many reasons, that never happened.

For years, I worked at clerical or administrative jobs. My focus was on my kids and my responsibility to provide for them, especially after my first divorce, when they were very small. I worked my way up through some pretty soul-sucking positions in places where I wasn't even liked. At different points, I worked for a murderer, an embezzler, and an abuser—three different men—as well as other, better people. I wore suits, pantyhose, costume jewelry, and short heels every day.

I never thought about having a passion for my job, about loving the place where I worked. I shot out of the office at the end of every day, eager to get to my real life, at home with my kids.

And then the internet happened, and CitySearch came to town. CitySearch was a venture-backed dot-com out of Silicon Valley. It was one of the first online city guides, like a newspaper on the web, with small websites for local businesses that we called "info-sites." Somehow, I understood this company intuitively, even though I'd only surfed the web one time before my interview. I got the job as marketing director for the Nashville office, which put me in the spotlight for this very popular company. We made tsunami-like waves, quickly.

(In fact, those waves were so large that it seemed everyone knew who we were. When I had to call the police to come to my house on one unfortunate night, as the officer was filling out a report, he asked for my place of employment. I said, "CitySearch." He looked at me and asked, "Dot-com?" Yes!)

My boss at CitySearch, Frank Condurelis, was an outgoing, loving guy. One of the truest things he ever said to me was, "When start-up gets in your blood, you'll never be able to go back to corporate America."

I didn't doubt him, but I didn't know he was, in that moment, being a prophet.

TRAJECTORY

There is a specific and predictable trajectory in the life of a business that experts write about all the time. Businesses move from the developmental stage to the start-up stage, then to growth, expansion, and, finally, to maturity, at varying rates. Business owners take their companies through those steps almost intuitively, leading from their gut, not knowing that they are transitioning to a new stage until it's done.

Most change is gradual; it's accomplished step by step, not in giant leaps. One day, you walk into your company and you just know that you are no longer a start-up. Another day, you go home and you realize that the expansion phase just ended. You watch as you lose your thoroughbred and realize you aren't the same company you were when she got there. You look mournfully at the mature company you've become and miss the start-up days.

I believe the trajectory I have described is right, but it is not a straight, smooth path from start-up to maturity. There is backtracking along the way, expansion followed by contraction. Business does not always increase. Sometimes you are forced to retrench.

It's by looking in the rear-view mirror that you identify why things got harder or better, why you instituted certain processes, why you shed some clients or employees, etc. Big changes are usually made out of pain, because it is a powerful motivator. Pain is what makes you push through the discomfort of big decisions and changes because, hopefully, relief is on the other side.

And usually it is. At least for a while.

As companies move toward maturity, they are forced to put structure and processes in place to solve the problems that growth brings. But when you solve one problem, you create others. Even though I understood the need for it, as an entrepreneurial, inspirational business owner, structure and process lessened my enjoyment of the business.

Our path from start-up to maturity was particularly difficult because of the industry we were in and the demographic makeup of our team. At the same time that I was building a business, the industry was also maturing, then splintering and mushrooming. Undoubtedly, digital is everywhere. Carving out a niche in this space was maddening. As soon as you thought you had it, another huge change crashed into your company.

In my rear-view mirror, I can now see a few big moves

that had a lasting impact on Paramore Digital. Who knows what would have happened had we not leaned into core values, focused on culture, instituted more processes, expanded into other cities, raised our profile, and broadened our offerings? With each of those decisions, we made some progress, but often not enough. Some decisions were absolute mistakes. Others had delayed benefits that were quite surprising.

Big decisions are never 100 percent right. They are neither solely good nor solely bad. They are a combination, and they are necessary and inevitable in any business.

Following are the major beliefs and decisions that drove change in Paramore Digital as we approached maturity and the effect they had on me as I attempted to lead the company day by day.

CORE VALUES

About three years into the business, I was challenged to write the core values of our company while taking a class through the Nashville Area Chamber of Commerce. The company was still very small at the time, with only four or five people, including me. Writing core values, which I associated with corporate America, for such a young, small company seemed silly to me, but I went with it. I had thirty minutes to complete the exercise and came out with this:

- Focused on Results: We care about the results of our work more than getting paid for it.

- Brilliant Finishes: We are as excited about your project at the end as we were at the beginning.
- 100 Percent Delivery: We deliver every point of every proposal.
- Doing the Right Thing: We recommend the right thing for our clients, not necessarily the thing that will make us the most money.
- Excellent Quality: We use industry best practices, even if our client doesn't know or care.
- Honor the Client: We treat the client with respect, even when they are not in the room.
- Respect for the Individual: We respect the personal time of our staff and don't require unreasonable hours on nights or weekends.
- Personal Responsibility: We each are responsible for the success of our company and growing our relationships with our clients.
- Transparency: We are transparent with our feelings, our ideas, and our business processes.

I sat back, looked at my list, and thought, well, that's a lot. But it was solid, and it lasted. With only a change of wording in two of them over time, those core values were essentially the same when I sold the company thirteen years later. They defined us.

Our employees were very loyal to the core values because we practiced them consistently. We kept them front and center. Drawing on my preacher genes, we would discuss one core value at a time in our Monday morning production meetings. We did exercises around them at our annual retreat. We painted them on the wall in our office. We included them in job descriptions and annual reviews.

I knew they had been fully embraced when I heard people using them to make decisions. They'd say things like, "How are we going to have a brilliant finish on this project?" or, "We have to deliver this even if we are over budget so we can have 100 percent delivery."

There was one core belief of mine—transparency—that was the heart and soul of the company and which did so much to make us successful. But that too became problematic as we grew, for one simple reason: we work with people, and each person is a unique individual. They bring to work their history, their beliefs, and their hopes for the future. They also bring prejudices, strengths and weaknesses, talents, disciplines, addictions, bad habits, and needs. They will embrace your messages and then twist them to fit their reality. Because they are people.

But, for the most part, core values are inspirational. They describe you on your very best day, like your dating profile. At their best, they align people around a set of principles and help you make decisions that streamline the decision-making process in a company. They enable your staff to move faster because they don't have to guess how you would handle most any situation.

At Paramore Digital, the Core Values became the basis of our culture.

CULTURE

Start-ups attract both employees and clients through their vision for something new and their relaxed, yet urgent, mission-oriented culture. I was long on both. I was determined to consistently live out the core values, and I was positive about two things: 1) traditional agencies didn't have the digital knowledge or expertise they needed to help their clients, and 2) most companies didn't have the budgets to attract big digital agencies such as Razorfish, so there was good market opportunity for us. I was born with a sense of urgency, and I brought it to work with me every day. Values, vision, and urgency—the holy trinity.

During my employment at CitySearch, I had learned what a motivated, enthusiastic team looked like and just how much a group could achieve together, so I set out to replicate what I'd experienced there: a relaxed, fun atmosphere; a team approach; flexibility; hard work; new, interesting ideas; no hierarchy; disco balls; a sense of purpose. And things went great. This type of culture was synonymous with the industry; it's sort of like the college dorm experience, with pizza boxes everywhere.

A culture-driven company can achieve great things quickly, especially in an emerging industry. The answer to almost every question in that stage is yes. Yes, we can turn our proposal around in twelve hours; we're making it up anyway. Yes, we can build that in six weeks; we'll just buy more pizza and eat at our desks. Yes, we can buy another ping pong table; we'll just do without a conference room. Yes, we'll sit on the floor if needed; we'd prefer a bean bag over an ergonomically correct desk chair anyway.

Everyone was all in. Every idea was at least considered. Work was so much fun, nobody wanted to go home.

Culture-driven companies rely principally on two things: an inspirational leader and fun. As long as you can fund the fun and inspire people to work for something beyond themselves, you just go and go and go.

Except that there's this thing called the second law of thermodynamics.

That law states that the universe tends toward disorder. An article published by *Farnam Street* titled "Entropy: The Hidden Force That Complicates Life"[2] describes it like this:

"As you read this article, entropy is all around you. Cells within your body are dying and degrading, an employee or coworker is making a mistake, the floor is getting dusty, and the heat from your coffee is spreading out. Zoom out a little, and businesses are failing, crimes and revolutions are occurring, and relationships are ending. Zoom out a lot further and we see the entire universe marching towards a collapse."

CULTURE SETS EXPECTATIONS AND, IF UNCHECKED, BECOMES UNSUSTAINABLE.

Uncontrolled disorder increases over time. The only way to push it back a bit is by applying energy. And yet, even energy tends toward disorder. You are quickly becoming ineffective.

If that is true, then the first law of culture might be this: culture sets expectations and, if unchecked, becomes unsustainable.

THE FLIP SIDE OF A CULTURE-DRIVEN COMPANY

What happened to us is that our culture definitely worked for us...until it worked against us. Starting out, I wanted to keep the freedom, fun, and focus in my day, to work only to the point that I was effective and then to go home. That sounds perfect, except for this fact: your young staff is looking to you to set the boundaries that will help them learn to be a good employee. They don't need to get everything they want. They must mature as people and as employees in order to be balanced, productive members of society. That requires discipline and high expectations alongside the nurturing, fun culture expected of almost every company today.

I also wanted to love my team and to express that love to them in ways that would matter to them personally. I wanted to do the unexpected, to consider the personality of the employee and do something for them that probably nobody else would ever do, like wowing them with gifts out of the blue. I've never been a fan of generic gifts; gifts should be personal, and they should be a surprise, something you need or want but wouldn't buy for yourself.

For example, I am not much on small talk in the office. I was glad people had great lives and friends in the office, but I didn't have time to get drawn into that as our staff grew. So, I disciplined myself not to join every conversation about weddings and babies, even though they are fun. Instead, when one of our ladies was getting married, I would take her to lunch the last week before her wedding and listen to all of her plans. I asked detailed questions. We had champagne. Then I would take her shopping at my favorite boutique and buy her wardrobe for her honeymoon.

For Christmas one year, I took my young, whip-smart account service director for a surprise shopping trip and bought her a season's worth of professional clothing.

I sent new appliances to one employee who was line-drying her clothes because their washer and dryer were broken, and her husband was between jobs.

We granted a three-day, flexible-hour workweek to the first woman who had a baby and wanted to come back to work.

We created event after event to acknowledge and celebrate even the smallest of successes. We made up holidays like Formal Wear Day every February 29th. We sent people to conferences and on client trips to go white water rafting and roller coaster riding.

We supported the arts, creating a rotating art gallery in our new office and inviting the artists in to talk to us about their inspiration and process. We also supported one major nonprofit, the YWCA of Nashville and Middle Tennessee, producing their biggest fundraiser of the year for six years in a row.

All of the generosities, personal touches, altruistic beliefs, and transparencies did exactly what I intended them to do by showing the team that they were loved and appreciated, and they returned that with dedication and hard work for the company.

It was wonderful at first, and then the staff grew, and I began to see that all this culture was setting unrealistic expectations. It wasn't actually producing the long-term result we'd hoped for. Turnover increased anyway.

Personal shopping trips became a thing of the past, tossed out in favor of equity in the workplace; it turns out that favoritism isn't a good thing. Allowing three-day, flexible work schedules is untenable when you have several new moms in the office. Having twenty to twenty-five millennials on staff who are entering the marriage and family years is also hard on your business. Our concessions grew and grew and became the norm, not the exception. We began to struggle to have a full team who were all at work at the same time. Scheduling became almost a full-time job. Events now were major expenses and cumbersome to plan and manage. Having ping pong tables in the conference room and dogs by their owners' sides ate into productivity instead of increasing it.

The joy and fun of the events started to slip away. It turns out that not everyone wants to go climb a fake rock wall on a Friday afternoon. Pleasing people with our fun ideas became an issue, so we tried harder.

Similar to the parent of a teenager who starts giving attitude for the first time, the entrepreneur tries to fix everything with the carrot but without the stick (because you can't use a stick at work), until you learn that, just like your teenager at home, employees are inherently ungrateful. What starts out as a perk quickly becomes an expectation, losing its ability to inspire and motivate.

That's enough to make even a good boss angry.

PROCESS

At eight years in business and with fifteen employees, we started to hurt. The Great Recession of 2008 took two years to stop by our place, and when it did, I wasn't sure what was happening. I saw our revenue, profit, and operating expenses all going in the wrong direction. Balls were dropping. People were turning over. We started to lose clients. We were entering the teenage years of our business and, just like teenagers, we needed some boundaries.

The first boundary came in the form of a legitimate project management system to help us manage the volume of work we were producing. The business had mushroomed, and we could not get by on the simplistic system we used randomly for some time. After months of input and weeks of training, we finally had a production process. I was excited. This promised to be the answer to our problems of accountability, work schedules, data, file storage, integrated billing, and financial reports.

I'll admit we needed all of that. But before too long, we had processes for our processes, and that's the first time I came off the rails at work. When I would ask for a quick status on a project, I started to hear things like, "I'll put it into production." I didn't even know what that meant.

On my way back into the office from a client meeting one day, I called an account manager to ask a question about a project, and he said, "Let me check the schedule. Yes, I am scheduled to talk to you about that tomorrow," and then sat quietly.

It's a good thing he was quiet, because then I didn't have to yell so loudly when I responded, "Why don't you talk to me about it *right now!*"

I noticed other things through the months. Instead of discussing a problem for a few minutes, then deciding, we had this process that had to be fed. Questions, data, and meetings were scheduled, and decisions all had to go through The Process and be entered there for some stupid reason. People started pointing fingers when something would go wrong. They'd say, "Well, it wasn't in the system."

I walked into the office with our development director one morning and said to him, "Hey! What are you working on today?"

His answer was, "I have no idea."

"What do you mean?" I asked him.

He said, "I don't know what I'm doing until the production manager hands me my task list."

This was exactly what I did not want in my company, and it was a signal that the start-up stage was ending. Suddenly, everybody wanted to have their day scheduled through the system rather than deal with people face to face.

Process becomes its own reality. Left unchecked, it becomes a monster that takes away the soulful moments among your team, like those stand-up meetings where we struggled to reach a decision point together. Those all-in brainstorming sessions where we came out with just the right idea. Your teammates jumping into a problem project with you for a few minutes to make it better.

The continual focus on process over people brought a negative vibe to our office. Process is rules-based. It focuses on time and money and data, not communication. It produces reports that tell only part of the story and teach you the wrong lessons. Without a leash on it, process produces a fear-based culture where your people are constantly looking for proof that a mistake wasn't their fault. You end up paying people to babysit a tool rather than collaborate with each other.

The process did give us information we didn't have before, and we tried to learn the right lessons from it. But the more we leaned into process, the less profitable we became. The hours spent tweaking and working around the tool sucked the lifeblood and profit out of the company.

A few months after selling Paramore Digital, I attended the New Work conference put on by *The New York Times*. Steelcase and Microsoft did one of the opening presentations, and they made this point that really resonated with me:

Every company today is trying to recapture the start-up vibe.

I think that's true. There is freedom and a surprising amount of efficiency in a company that just *goes* without a lot of process. A company that is truly open-door policy. Truly team oriented. Truly all about impact, not hours. You move fast, and everybody has direct access to decision makers. I thought about that as I listened to the presenters talk about the path from start-up to grown-up.

The presenters went on to say that start-ups either fail or succeed. When they succeed, they establish processes. Then they wish they were a start-up again.

At Paramore, after we reached the place we thought we wanted to be, with a new office and larger profile, I started to hear remarks about how Paramore "used to be." We had a beautiful office with the space we needed to grow, but people were whining that "we're so disconnected now." There's no pleasing 'em.

It's definitely more fun to be a teenager than a grown-up.

LEVELING UP

The adage, "If you're not growing, you're dying," is stamped into the prefrontal cortex of all entrepreneurs. It's touted as true, and you're made to feel that if you don't believe it, you're doomed. But I don't believe it's true.

It *is* true that nothing stays the same and that as driven people, we continually strive to learn and to grow. In the early years of a business, growth is natural and not all that risky. You have nowhere to go but up. But there are critical moments in your business when you are faced with the chance to either grow or not, to expand to meet the opportunities you are getting through your client relationships and reputation in the community or not. That kind of growth gets riskier as the years go by.

We faced it in 2014 after twelve years in business. We had not replaced our big client loss. We also were transitioning out of our second largest client and were on the cusp, unbeknownst to us, of losing the client that was now our largest after the loss we'd experienced in 2013.

We wrote our strategic plan for the next year around the ideas "Go Big" and "Go Broad." We wanted to grow client relationships to encompass traditional media work as well as digital. Client opportunities were leading us there. We also had major pitches coming up that pushed us in that direction. Our team was maturing and wanted to continue to broaden their skills to sit in the driver's seat with clients. We had two VPs in remote offices who handled business development and provided senior leadership to our Nashville team. With another key hire out of traditional marketing, we were set with senior talent who had broad and deep experience both at Paramore and elsewhere.

We had just moved to the most prestigious corner in downtown Nashville, and our name, my daddy's name, was on the top of the building, complete with a smartphone app that would allow anyone in the world to change the color of the sign from anywhere in the world. Our profile was big and growing. We were a part of the scene.

So, we went for it. And we were frustrated with the results.

Even though we did cross over to traditional marketing with some clients, it wasn't enough, and we saw some negative consequences as a result of this effort. Our competitive set changed. We were targeted by bigger competitors, and they fought harder to keep their relationships with clients. Staff unrest seemed to escalate. When you paint a picture of a potentially rosier future and you don't reach it, it's hard on the team. They don't want to go backward.

It seems natural that if you've been successful in a niche, you should be able to broaden and be even more successful. But strategy shifts have a real cost, both financially and with opportunity, and carry with them a risk that you don't initially see. So, you hire for the new skillset. You begin to redirect your team to think of things differently. You show up differently in the community. You suffer revenue attrition from the deals you would have gone after if you hadn't changed your focus. You start to underperform on your core expertise. Your staff grows weary of working on the "old clients."

And it's downright disappointing to not win all the time. Your team feels the sting of loss, maybe for the first time, and doubt creeps in.

There is no success without risk but understanding the tangible and intangible risks of a market strategy shift is important and not something a young team understands. In fact, I was shocked at how difficult things were during this period. We couldn't find the partnership opportunities we'd had in the past. There was a resistance from other agencies to work with us. We weren't as successful closing smaller business because we looked too big. Conversely, we weren't big enough to close major accounts; their appetites were now for agencies outside of Nashville as our industry splintered and grew and became even more confusing for the buyer.

The disappointment from this two-year period led to panic as we began to fail at projects we'd never struggled with in the past. Taking our eye off the customers that had made us successful led us to a difficult place.

But it wasn't all bad. We were still profitable during that period, but our profit was on a steady downhill slide. What would happen in the years after proved that this effort was not wasted, but those moments were painful and led straight to Ambien Day.

TRANSPARENCY

Back when I first joined CitySearch.com, I was sent to the home office in Pasadena for a few days of orientation. In the middle of the afternoon on one of the days I was there, a horn sounded, and everyone got up from their desk and made their way to a large empty section of the office. At that time, the company took up a couple of floors in the office building, but with the exception of several small rooms in the center core where two to three people could gather for a private conversation, the rest of the floor had no walls. Everyone sat at makeshift desks pushed together or corralled around stuffed animals or concrete poles. One part of the floor had no desks at all, and that's where everyone headed when the horn sounded.

I was amazed as everyone sat on the floor and listened to Charles Conn, the founder, give an update on what had happened in the previous week. He was engaging. Inspirational. There was popcorn. He answered questions, and then, after about eighteen minutes, everyone dispersed and went back to work.

I'd just experienced my first all-company meeting. I was changed.

As I mentioned previously, we had nine core values at Paramore Digital, beginning with Focused on Results and ending with Transparency.

Although Transparency was the last one listed, it was the one that morphed, changed shape, and grew deeper over time. I initially meant for it to describe the clarity on the scope of work, billing, communication, etc., that our clients would experience when working with us. But it became so much more. It set the stage for the openness with which I shared with the staff almost everything about the company. There was a direct line of benefit from the company's success to the employee's bonus at the end of the year, so I thought that if the team understood how the company made money, they would be more focused on doing business right and helping the company to succeed. I taught them the math of the business: how we put together estimates, what the profit on each piece of business was (or should be), and how all of that flowed to the bottom line. As their knowledge and our experience with clients and projects grew, we had conversations about the type of client we wanted. We learned to spot a good potential client and to see the issues with a marginal one. We became savvier at having tough conversations with clients when projects started to go sideways. I started to feel less alone in decision-making and teaching the staff how to run a business was some of the most fun I had during those fifteen years.

Showing employees the math of the business was the right thing to do; it opened up decision-making and made putting together budgets and talking about project parameters easier. But it also opened up an ugly can of worms. It was too easy for an employee to look at the hourly rate we were charging and then do the math on their salary. With no understanding of what it takes to build a profitable business, they felt cheated. That feeling gave way to discontent, which resulted in bad attitudes, stalled projects, and, finally, turnover.

The people who stayed took to thinking about themselves and their needs more than the team as a whole. In an open culture such as ours, what you want to achieve is alignment so that everyone understands the end game for the business, what the client needs, and how doing good work is good for everybody, including the employee. When the team is tight—as in, made up of no more than fifteen people—true alignment is easier to achieve. Past that, however, it is exponentially harder. There are always one or two people who aren't as connected to the mission of the company, and they have a huge impact on the culture.

Each person that comes into a group changes the group.

If your group is larger than fifteen people and you have a flat organization, you simply cannot communicate enough to keep everyone on the same page. Factions develop. Turf wars start. Expectations become skewed, and the focus is no longer on pulling together to do the right thing for the client and the company. The staff is primarily concerned with how each decision effects them. When you realize this, you formalize a layer of management between you and the staff, and that is when you cross over. You are no longer a start-up.

The flip side of an open culture drove me into madness. Openness invites dialogue, which devolves into dissent. The more open I was about the opportunities and challenges we faced, the more the staff thought they should have a say in decisions, particularly about which clients we accepted and when we should resign them. The underlying expectation was that the work would always be fun, and we'd only work for companies we liked. The staff could not accept that sometimes work is just work. When we disagreed, they would cite the core values in defense of their position. That created a conflict inside me; I loved that they were applying the core values, but I hated that they were using them to defend a position that was only half informed.

Just like with other communication challenges, I learned that as you grow, you can only be so open in an open culture. A young staff does not have the life experience, patience, or business acumen to understand how many hard decisions an owner must make. If you shared with them all that is involved in business ownership and the tenuous nature of almost every business today—from salaries to new business pitches to office leases and finances—they'd be paralyzed by fear and uncertainty. At the end of the day, it's not their business. They have no skin in the game and no long-term commitment to the company. They can leave. And they do.

It makes you want to take it all back.

THE LONG AND WINDING ROAD

Like most entrepreneurs, I'm an open person. I like to share and collaborate. The best path from here to there is inclusive, bringing together a variety of opinions and talents. Getting people's input helps make an idea better, builds excitement and buy-in, and is the only way to get a team to really produce. As your company is moving through the different stages of growth and maturity, encountering hurdles along the way, having a team that is all moving in the same direction is so important...it's just not easy. It's not a straight path; it's a long and winding road.

Walking that line as the business owner is one of the hardest things you will do. How much do you share with your team? Whose opinion do you seek on big decisions? How many people can you trust?

These questions were particularly hard for me because of the demographic of the Paramore team. Their youth added so much to the success of the company, but when it came to making big decisions or dealing with critical issues, their youth was a hindrance.

But I didn't want it to be, so I kept trying, thinking that if I could cast the right vision, reward the right behavior, remove the right barriers, the team would be motivated to help the company succeed. After fifteen years of chasing those ideals, I finally learned something...

Motivation is internal.

You cannot actually motivate a team to do anything. Motivation comes from somewhere deep within a person. Whether a person is committed to your company or not is much more about who they are and where they are in their life than what you are doing for them as their boss. Their motivation shapes their input at work, which means that their contributions to a project could be for their own benefit, not for the company's. For instance, if they're motivated by career progression, they could focus on shaping a project so that it looks good on their resumé, regardless of the client's needs. Or, if they're motivated by perfection, they could spend much more time than the company is being paid for to get a project to their satisfaction. These actions are driven by selfish motivation. It's about them, not the client, and certainly not the company.

> **WHETHER A PERSON IS COMMITTED TO YOUR COMPANY OR NOT IS MUCH MORE ABOUT WHO THEY ARE AND WHERE THEY ARE IN THEIR LIFE THAN WHAT YOU ARE DOING FOR THEM AS THEIR BOSS.**

As the business owners, we cannot know what our team's motivation is, so we spend time trying to solve the wrong problem. We put processes and procedures in place. We shift the strategy to match the type of work the team wants to do rather than what the market is calling for. We share more and more with the team, looking for the thing that will motivate them to behave the way the company needs them to.

Inspiration, on the other hand, is external, and it's where you can make a difference with your team. People want their leader to be inspirational. They want to believe that they are contributing to something bigger than themselves. For a small business owner whose main responsibility is the health of their small company, it's hard to consistently inspire a team toward both macro and micro issues. My way of doing that was to teach the basis of how a business stays in business. That strategy had both positive and negative consequences. If you overshare, trust the wrong people, or include too many people in decisions, you have one problem. If you rein it in, you have another.

It is all trial and error, because you do not know what will happen once you unleash information. The constant struggle to help people understand—and do the right thing with—the information they are given is, in turn, both encouraging and discouraging.

The long and winding road in a business, from start to finish, is treacherous.

---

1 https://sbecouncil.org/about-us/facts-and-data/

2 https://fs.blog/2018/11/entropy/

KEY TAKEAWAYS

1. There is a flip side to everything.

- Every good thing you do for your company will have a flip side. Be intentional.
- Consider how the information you share or an idea you implement will scale when you don't know each person in your company intimately.

2. Core values are essential.

- Be stringent in your adherence to core values. Use them every day. Make them a part of job descriptions, annual reviews, training, weekly meetings, etc.

3. Process.

- Instilling process in a creative company can cut into the soul of the company and change you. Be careful how much process you embrace. Focus on results over data. When you have to institute a process, find detail-oriented people who value communication as much as data to implement the solution.

4. Next-level stuff is hard.

- It takes more than one year to make a strategic change in your business. Be careful to set the expectation correctly in your budgets and with your staff.

5. Business growth is not a straight path.

- Accept the setbacks. Play for the long game. Don't panic.
- Join an accountability group. Seek out mentors. Visit the competition. Learn everything you can about business ownership and the path your company will take in your industry.

— CHAPTER FIVE —

ME

KNOW THYSELF

I'm glad you are still reading. By now, you may think that I'm just a whiner, or that I blame everybody else for my pain, or that I'm ungrateful when the situation actually worked out pretty well for me...I sold my business, and now I caddy for my husband, Bill Breen, who is not only a good golfer but a very good-looking man, too.

But here's the thing: I loved owning Paramore Digital. I was in my sweet spot. It was the professional mountaintop for me. I couldn't wait to get into the office every day. Minor holidays (Independence Day, Memorial Day, Labor Day) annoyed me, because I hated taking the time off. Even major holidays were a problem. I couldn't figure out why people felt like they needed both Christmas *and* New Year's off when we had so much fun, exciting work to do!

Even the challenges were electrifying for me. I was

never afraid, even when we lost big clients or talented people. I was 100 percent confident we would succeed. The busyness of the company masked the problems that bubbled underneath the surface for years, but I worked with mostly wonderful people. I loved them, and they loved me back. While I complain—a lot—about millennials, I'm also in awe of them. They are the future, and they are changing the world.

But during my last three years at Paramore, things just felt off to me. For twelve years, I had led the company with confidence. Even during the toughest times, when I was calling in consultants and therapists, I did not have the sense that doom was lurking just around the corner. In fact, in the last year before the acquisition, the people I talked to about my fear looked at me a little sideways when they heard my despair. They saw a successful business with a strong leader, but I saw something else. While things looked good from the outside, they felt horrible on the inside.

But why? None of the facts of the business had actually changed. We were still in an emerging industry. We were still profitable. We still attracted strong talent. We still had A-list clients. We had a high-profile office and a high-profile leader.

What, then?

Quite simply, I changed. After more than a decade of leading the company and moving from challenge to opportunity as an optimistic, aggressive leader, I suddenly felt vulnerable. That vulnerability turned into disillusionment. At the end, I was disengaged. I became afraid to manage the business.

VULNERABILITY

From 2002 through 2016, as my business was moving from start-up to maturity, I was also maturing as a business owner. At first, the learning curve was energizing. I craved it. But the more I learned, the more the truth of business ownership began to emerge. In a perfect example of entropy in the middle of success, other people all around me were making decisions that hurt the company. Employees were turning in their notice. Clients were listening to our competition criticize our work. Wages, taxes, and benefit costs were increasing. I was becoming less effective in the business.

For years, I had been constantly adjusting, absorbing one issue and one loss after another. At first, I did so with confidence. But eventually, years of defending our work, fighting to win and keep clients, getting staff in the right place—and then losing them anyway—wears you down, and one day I realized that it would never, ever stop. I saw myself alone, the only person committed to the business, the only person with anything—everything—to lose. I felt vulnerable.

Vulnerability is a wonderful thing in personal relationships. It also works when you are growing your team, fostering a deeper commitment from the staff. But this was a different kind of vulnerability. This vulnerability warned that great loss was just around the corner, and I was helpless to stop it. Whether it makes any sense or not, that was the feeling I had. I couldn't get out of my mind the advice that business books and consultants tell you, that if you're not growing, you're dying. It felt like we were dying.

I SAW MYSELF ALONE, THE ONLY PERSON COMMITTED TO THE BUSINESS,

I was paralyzed with fear. If we didn't replace those clients, what would happen to the company? We were still closing business but, mirroring the industry, work had slipped from agency of record contracts to smaller projects. The lease on the new office, the large staff ready to take on more work, the moves we'd made to propel us forward, all of that depended on having two to three large clients in the mix. But they weren't coming.

I began to slowly fall apart. The words of my team didn't make any sense to me anymore. I mean, they were speaking English, but I couldn't understand what they were saying. I had no witty or smart answers to normal questions. I couldn't process information or respond at all. I checked out in the middle of conversations. Everything was fuzzy. I couldn't hear, couldn't speak. Had nothing to say.

You cannot do the right thing for your business when you have that much fear. We had embraced transparency, but it's hard to tell the staff that you are out of ideas and you really need them to *save the company*. They look to you for the confidence that everything will be all right. They think you have the answers. When you don't, they get scared, and that unease becomes a self-fulfilling prophecy. Fear is contagious, and your staff is rightfully concerned about how this uncertainty will affect them. They start to take those phone calls from recruiters. The positive vibe in the company is gone. The clients feel it too and start to take calls from your competitors.

For the business owner, when things get critical, there is nowhere to turn. You can't take your fears to the leadership team, and you certainly can't reveal them to the staff. Even mentors are limited in their ability to understand and help guide you through the trough, because they are not in your business every day.

As we fought to rebound in 2014, I began to feel like a failure. My confidence was gone, and I could not get it back. It leaked over to the leadership team and then to the staff. Our work became shaky. Soon, in addition to the feeling of vulnerability, there was disillusionment.

DISILLUSIONMENT

You need the same skill to build a successful business that you do to enjoy a Sylvester Stallone movie: you have to suspend disbelief. Suspending disbelief means that you do not believe the company can possibly fail. At all. You're able to ride the waves, enjoying the story as it plays out, not worrying about the way it will all end. That's confidence, and it's what attracts people.

The CEO's confidence in the business is everything.

Once it's gone, it's over.

As the years went by and we transitioned from one phase to the next, everything we did became more difficult. My confidence in our ability to produce excellent work faded. Our company philosophy had always been: Simple, Clear, and Focused on Results. That promise is what clients bought. For years, we simplified every project in order to get to the heart of the strategy and produce the right thing for the client. But by 2012, the clients' appetites for something they perceived as cutting edge and the staff's desire to expand their skills, combined with the complexities of the industry, encumbered every project with multiple problems. To complete the project and satisfy the client, we'd end up losing money. If we actually made money, the client wasn't satisfied, and the staff was bored. For the first time, Brilliant Finishes seemed beyond our reach. Actually, *finishing* seemed beyond our reach. There were problems during the launches, a post-launch list that went on for weeks, discontent at the end of every project, and one media campaign after another that lost money for our company. The agency team would limp across the finish line with resentment over how the client made them feel as they tried to do the right thing, both honoring the client and protecting the agency's bottom line. No matter how good the quality of the work really was or how great the results were for the client, everybody was disappointed all the time.

My job had become managing disappointment. It was hard to find something to celebrate.

Business owners look to different aspects of their businesses to bolster themselves when things get tough. If your staff is in turmoil, you look to the client relationship to find satisfaction and support. If the client relationship is suffering, you look to the staff for ingenuity to stay in the game. When both are troublesome, you look to the industry for encouragement. When I looked there, however, I got hives.

By mid-2014, not only was I disillusioned with my company and our ability to produce consistently good work, I was disillusioned with the whole idea of owning a business. Everything was more expensive. Obamacare hit our group of young, healthy millennials in their child-bearing years hard. The Fair Labor Standards Act (FLSA) threat of 2016 drove me out of my mind. We seemed to be the only business that couldn't raise its rates. Mounting competition and confusion in the market made it very hard to pass on the increased cost of doing business to the client. Instead, we took it on our bottom line. Owning a business started to feel like a stupid idea.

DISENGAGED LEADER

Whining again. I know that's what you are thinking. But listen, I know that if I'd done a few things before 2013, I would have been able to lead us back to our happy place. Instead, I became death to the business. I became the picture of the disengaged employee.

I stopped thinking about the long-term. Instead, I

started playing not to lose, which, as it turns out, is part of the natural aging process. In my late 50s by then, I felt differently about everything than I had in my early 40s; money, time, hobbies, and interests were all different for me. At this stage of life, if you bet wrong, there is less time to recover. You're more sensitive about wasting time because most of your life is behind you. Things that used to be so important to you are just not significant any longer. You judge the value of everything differently.

My interest in our work also changed. By this time, all of the clients and their business problems looked the same to me. Work became less interesting when I realized we were solving the same problem for one client after another. And I trusted the clients less, because even if we solved their problem, they would still leave.

I've been surrounded by elderly people a good bit during the last several years, and I've noticed that while some of them are still active and current in their grasp of society and their contribution to it, many of them live in the past. They tell and retell the stories from their youth, drawing the same lesson from those stories each time. It's endearing, but also frustrating to the listener. Eventually, I found myself doing the equivalent during those last three years at Paramore. My examples were less relevant. My observations were based on the first few years of the business. My vision for the future wasn't very specific. My skills began to age out, and I was no longer involved in much client work. I began to question my value to the company.

In this downward spiral, panic set in. The staff and leadership team clamped down to prove they were still busy and valuable to the company. The work slowed down. There were protracted meetings about decisions that would have been no-brainers in the past. Small process issues became insurmountable problems. Fear walked in and sat down in every meeting, a tangible presence. Disillusionment greeted me every morning.

When my company needed me to lead, I could no longer do so because I didn't value my own leadership.

Everyone has a limit. I was done. I didn't have anything to give the business anymore.

A NEW VISION

For years, I'd felt alone in the business. I yearned for a partner to share the good and the bad, to relieve the burden, to bring perspective and balance. In 2014, I found him, but not for my business—for my life. When Paramore hit its toughest days, my personal life took a turn for the better. I fell in love with my golf pro, Bill Breen, who brought with him a family that is larger than life. They actually expect you to show up for birthdays and holidays, both major and minor. They write thank-you notes. They bring their truck to help you move furniture. They take you to the airport. They call to find out if you've arrived safely. Suddenly, at every speech I gave, I'd have family in the audience. They show up to everything you invite them to.

The contrast was incredible, the change of heart almost

immediate. I could not, could not, *could not* work at night on a proposal or attend another networking event when my mother-in-law, Barbara, was cooking dinner. I could not make another trip to see a far-flung client when there was a Saturday Skins Game with Bill. I could not miss a golf tournament for a leadership meeting.

At the same time my, children were building families. I now had six grandchildren entering interesting years. My parents were both aging, their days more precious to me now.

They say that nature abhors a vacuum, that as soon as a space opens up in your life, nature conspires to fill it. I believe that. As my business left my heart, my family showed up, and, quickly following, the chance to sell my business.

> ## AS MY BUSINESS LEFT MY HEART, MY FAMILY SHOWED UP, AND, QUICKLY FOLLOWING, THE CHANCE TO SELL MY BUSINESS.

Still, letting go was painful. I felt like I did back in 1976 when my family was imploding: like I was standing on a precipice and that one small move would send me over the edge into the abyss. It must be how a teenage girl feels the moment before she says, "Mom, I'm pregnant." Or how a man feels just before he asks, "Will you marry me?" What follows is unknown. It could be the best or the worst outcome. Either way, your life is on the brink of change.

Several years ago, a friend of mine invited me to join her for the regular Sunday Afternoon Jazz event that happens every week at a local restaurant. This incredible gathering has been taking place for close to thirty years now. It's three hours of Dixieland jazz performed by some of the best musicians in the business whose names you wouldn't recognize. They're behind the scenes, the quintessential studio musicians for which Nashville is famous. The group is loosely organized by the regulars, those folks who have been attending for these past thirty years. Many of them are now in their 90s, most of them women whose husbands used to attend with them but have now passed. For three hours every Sunday, they request songs and then applaud and wave their white napkins in excitement when the band swings into their favorites. Some weeks, we dance a slow, careful, but joyful promenade around that small room to the strains of "Panama."

I love all of the thirty or so people who attend, but I have my favorites. Gail, Byrd, and Billie became important to me as Bill and I were thinking about dating. They gave me advice that would change my life. They also gave me a great life lesson one night, when I was there with my father, who was visiting from North Carolina. As we left, Billie and Byrd were sitting by the door waiting for their ride, and we stopped to talk for a minute. I was explaining to Dad who they were, how they knew each other, and what their careers had been like when Byrd said, "Billie and I have the unusual distinction of having sat in each other's living rooms after the deaths of our daughters. And then we went to jazz and we found out there's a whole lot of life after a funeral."

Those simple words gave me the courage I needed to mourn the "death" of my business and know that there would be life afterward. In my heart, I knew it was time to sell my business because the pain of owning it had displaced the joy of having it. It was no longer worth the risk and the stress and the sleepless nights. I lost interest in it. I was angry every day at the office full of good people who came in and did their best. I had fallen in love with a vision of another kind of life, and I wanted to spend my days differently.

I knew it was time to sell my business because I wasn't the right person to lead it into the future. I had to admit that, during that last three years, I had become the limiting factor in the business. I realized that if I had solved some of the problems of the business earlier, I wouldn't be in that place emotionally. But I had to admit that for me, it was too late to solve those problems.

I didn't have a specific vision for what I would do professionally after Paramore, but I realized that would come when I was finally finished, and not a minute sooner. So, I took the plunge.

I hadn't been without a paycheck since I was twenty years old. I hadn't been without a team for fifteen years. I couldn't imagine how such a life could be, but, as I signed the papers to sell my company, I clung to the hope that there is a whole lot of life after business.

THE BUCK STOPS HERE

That buck that I've been passing actually stops right here. I've tried to explain through these pages what makes a person willing to sell a company they have created and loved. Some people do it because they have another business idea they want to pursue. Some do it because of personal or family dynamics such as a major illness. Some do it simply for the money. None of those were the case for me.

I did it to stop the pain. And yet, there were things I could have done that, had I known their importance, might have changed the outcome for me. It might have kept the fear and pain at bay and allowed me to make decisions about the future of the company, and my role in it, from a much better place; a place where I recognized that I had a *choice*.

The freedom to choose, whether it's how we worship or where we live or what we eat or how we work, is a basic human need. It's built into our DNA. We exercise this freedom even as babies when we refuse to nap when our mothers want us to or eat the creamed peas our parents serve us. We yearn for this freedom as teenagers when we resent the world and its pressure and structure. We hold onto it as adults when we encounter harassment at work or abuse at home. We choose not to stay where we are not safe. We thrive as we choose the kind of business we will create.

And then we feel trapped by the business we've created. We become afraid, and we stop choosing.

The process of selling my business was one of the two most stressful things I've ever been through in my life. Because I was in such a negative space emotionally when acquisition discussions began, I felt trapped. When you feel trapped, you react out of fear, not out of strength, and this changes everything. It could be the best deal in the world, but you will still feel cheated because you feel trapped. It could be the worst deal in the world, but you will feel like you have to take it because you feel trapped.

If I'd taken some critical steps and made some hard decisions years earlier, I could have preserved the *freedom to choose* as I negotiated the biggest deal of my life. The freedom to choose is the game changer. It displaces all panic and fear and opens the door to options. It puts you in the driver's seat and gives you the ability to walk away from something that makes you feel bad because you can walk toward the opposite: something that makes you feel good.

I don't know if the outcome would have been better, but if I had acted from the basis of choice rather than the fear of failure, there's no telling what might have happened.

KEY SUGGESTIONS

1. Find a way to keep the business interesting for yourself.

If you don't, eventually you won't do the right thing for the company. How do you keep things interesting? You research the next opportunity, or perhaps change your role to keep yourself in the right position. Owners are just people. We change too, and our role in the company needs to evolve as we change. Sometimes this may mean shifting your responsibilities. It also could mean shifting the vision and direction of the company so that it remains relevant to you.

2. Develop interests outside the company.

Find a hobby that you are so passionate about that you get impatient when work takes you away from it. It will round you out and make you build a structure that is not dependent on you being tied to the business five days a week (or more). For me, this was golf.

3. Take a sabbatical every five years. Have your VPs do the same.

At minimum, give yourself a three-month sabbatical. Six months would be even better. Spend it researching other business opportunities, resting, spending time with family, or pursuing your hobbies. And yes, continue to pay yourself during the sabbatical. I yearned for a sabbatical during the last few years of the business but always talked myself out of it. My burnout might have been avoidable had I allowed myself the time to rest and renew.

4. Find your number two.

Find the person who wants to be the CEO of your company, at almost whatever cost. Fear and disbelief kept me from doing this. The fear came from the risk to the company of a wrong hire and the hard cost of recruiting and paying this person, as well as the potential reaction from the team when someone new is brought in over them. I was afraid it would demotivate them and mess up the successful mix we'd achieved through years of promoting from within. I also didn't believe it was that important. The end result was that I burned out my young team and myself because I didn't have the senior partner I needed.

5. Take the blinders off regarding your biggest clients and their commitment to you.

There are almost always signs that clients are drifting. Look ruthlessly at those signs, and don't let a big client resignation be a surprise to you. Don't rely on your young leadership team to pick up on those signals. They don't have the years of experience it takes to know what's really happening.

6. Study your industry closely and shift your business model when industry changes dictate.

Stay in touch with changes in your industry that impact your business model. Understand where the industry is going, not where it is right now. Find like-minded business owners in your industry and get to know them. Learn from them.

I failed in this area by not accepting that development had changed. We locked ourselves into a model of building everything we sold internally rather than finding resources outside the company who could provide bench strength on an as-needed basis.

— CHAPTER SIX —

AFTER

The moment I told the Paramore team I had sold the business was just as hard as I thought it would be. People came to support me through it: my husband, Bill Breen, my PR agent, Lauren Reed, my accountant, Bill Easley. We had some time in my office alone. I was shaking, near tears, as I walked into the conference room where the entire Paramore staff was waiting for me.

The night before had been brutal. The last conference call with the buyer and attorneys on both sides almost broke me. I talked with Bill Easley after the call that night, asking him to have checks for each employee ready for the next morning—a bonus for each of them to thank them for their work, which made this sale possible. He'd been with me all fifteen years. As I asked him to write a check for himself, I began to weep.

His voice even broke a bit as he said, "It's just hitting you now, isn't it? It'll be alright. You've done good. Won't be long until you're into something else. We'll do it again."

I looked around at the office I had created only three years before. I loved it, and I feared it. Moving into it hadn't been the triumph I'd thought it would be because of the client we lost the day we moved in. I'd never relaxed and just simply enjoyed it. But it was beautiful, a real jewel.

The artwork, each piece specially chosen. Much of it would come home with me when I moved out a year later. The desk I'd had for ten years would stay. The disco ball, which I'd purchased for my first dot-com job at CitySearch and was hanging in the party area outside the main conference room, is also still there. The brass bell we rang with each signature. The gong we banged at each project launch. The rooftop deck. The sign bearing my name on top of the building.

I'd walked to this office every day. It had been the backdrop for many meetings and special occasions: client meetings, staff parties, holiday celebrations, community transit meetings, and, most importantly, mine and Bill's wedding reception. It was an extension of me, and I would leave it all behind.

I didn't know if I could do it.

Most of the staff was surprised. I tried, unsuccessfully, to hold back the tears as I broke the news. I focused on the positive aspects of the transaction as I saw the shock on their faces. The sense of loss in the room was palpable.

Feeling my pain, many of them also had tears in their eyes. It was so hard to get through the announcement.

And then, I had three hours to call a list of clients before the news story broke in the local and national media. I started with the easier ones, practicing up for the conversations that would be tougher. It wasn't perfect, but it wasn't as bad as I thought it would be. I explained the transition plan. Most congratulated me.

My buyer lived up to their word. The money arrived.

Most deals like this don't actually make it across the finish line. Either something happens in due diligence or one of the parties doesn't really have the stomach for it. Because of that, you never count on the deal closing until the money is in the bank, which makes it hard to plan a party. So, that night, although you'd think I'd have had a blow-out party since that is my style, instead we just had drinks and appetizers with Bill Easley and his wife, Simone and Pat and Lindsey, two friends of ours who were kind enough to change their schedules at the last minute. Selling Paramore was a big deal to me, but not to very many other people in the civilized world.

Everything was different immediately. The most foreign part was the shift in mindset from doing the right thing for the company to doing what I had to do to make sure I got my payout over the next two years. Those two things aren't completely inconsistent, but at times it's unclear how they live together. The bottom line is that an ex-owner isn't an owner. You're something else. Your focus has shifted.

AN EX-OWNER ISN'T AN OWNER. YOU'RE SOMETHING ELSE. YOUR FOCUS HAS SHIFTED.

For the next few months, I tried to figure out what to do. The repositioning of an owner/CEO is tough. Some people probably do it better than I did. Though I tried my best to contribute, it was unnatural in every way. Used to being busy beyond words, I now waited for somebody to pay attention to me, to expect something from me. It never happened.

My staff didn't know what to do with me now. They expected me to know the answers to the many questions they had. As they began to realize that I didn't, their focus began to shift, as it should. At first, I saw the conflict in their eyes, but it dimmed as time went by. I watched the shape of the company shift as people came and went, feeling less attachment with each change. My time in the office began to decline, until it was no longer necessary for me to show up at all. The business was continuing on, without me.

My dad once told me that leaving a place is like taking your hand out of a bucket of water. The water is disturbed for a while. It ripples and swirls around the hole your hand has left. But pretty soon the ripples stop, the gap closes, and the water smooths over, as if you were never there.

It sounds sad, doesn't it? But it's not. It's actually hopeful and positive. It means that we are all geared toward growth, toward moving forward. We are supposed to focus on the future, not on the past. Even our companies, if we build them right, will look toward the future after we leave them. When they do, it means we've built successful companies.

> **MY DAD ONCE TOLD ME THAT LEAVING A PLACE IS LIKE TAKING YOUR HAND OUT OF A BUCKET OF WATER. THE WATER IS DISTURBED FOR A WHILE. IT RIPPLES AND SWIRLS AROUND THE HOLE YOUR HAND HAS LEFT. BUT PRETTY SOON THE RIPPLES STOP, THE GAP CLOSES, AND THE WATER SMOOTHS OVER, AS IF YOU WERE NEVER THERE.**

You don't want the place to fall apart when you leave it. But in the moment, when the water is rippling and your hand still holds traces of the past you are leaving behind, it is painful.

I am thankful for the time I spent as a business owner, but I'm glad I didn't know ahead of time the struggles and pain that I would endure. If I had, I'd have been too scared to do it all. Which would have been a shame, because owning a business changed my life. It gave me the opportunity to stretch myself, and then to give myself away. It gave me a way to impact the world through the lives of people who would work for me and the clients whose businesses we would help succeed.

And finally, it led me to golf and to my future. Perhaps it's best that I don't know what's ahead there either. The greatest stuff of life is in the surprises, the twists and turns and joy and sorrow that you can't predict. It's in living it one moment at a time, making one decision after another with guiding principles to order those steps.

If you own a business now, I hope this cautionary tale doesn't scare you, but rather tells you that you are not alone in any of your feelings of hope and despair and uncertainty and fear. It is all normal. We are all normal. Do the next right thing. That's all.

I hope you have the time of your life. I hope I do, too.

— CORE VALUES —

HOW WE DO THE WORK

- **Focused on Results:** We care about the results of our work more than getting paid for it.
- **Brilliant Finishes:** We are as excited about your project at the end as we were at the beginning.
- **100 Percent Delivery:** We deliver every point of every proposal.
- **Doing the Right Thing:** We recommend the right thing for our clients, not necessarily the thing that will make us the most money.
- **Excellent Quality:** We use industry best practices, even if our client doesn't know or care.

HOW WE TREAT PEOPLE

- **Honor the Client:** We treat the client with respect, even when they are not in the room.
- **Respect for the Individual:** We respect the personal time of our staff and don't require unreasonable hours on nights or weekends.

HOW WE RUN THE BUSINESS

- **Personal Responsibility:** We each are responsible for the success of our company and growing our relationships with our clients.
- **Transparency:** We are transparent with our feelings, our ideas, and our business processes.

— AUTHOR NOTES —

I've worked out with a personal trainer, Dan Defigio, for many years. He sees my body in a way that nobody else sees it; like that my hips aren't exactly level and that my ears aren't over my shoulders no matter how much I argue with him. Unfortunately, all the common sense, basic workout things he tried to tell me for years turned out to be true as I approached 60. Like, that rows with weights are one of the things I need to do most because we stay hunched over everything every day. And that I had so many problems with pain in my neck and shoulders because I had a job that kept my shoulders up around my ears all the time. I denied all those things for so long, thinking they were standard answers to common complaints, but then I sold my business and those aches and pains started to disappear.

I tried to write this book right after the acquisition was finished in 2016. I had so much to say! But it did not happen. It was just too soon. Working through the first two chapters, Ambien Day and The Staff, were so emotional that I just lay, spent, on the floor for a while after I'd write a few paragraphs. The next two years were a confusion of trying to figure out where I should focus my time and how to transition out of a 24/7 ownership mentality to something else, whatever that would end up being.

The night before I closed the sale of my business, I was talking with Darwin Melnyk who first introduced me to my future buyers. I was, at that moment, fit to be tied as my grandmother would have said. It was November 29, 2016. Darwin advised me to take a breath, sign the papers, and relax in December. He said to show up ready to listen and be positive in January. He told me that it would take six months for me to realize I'd sold my business.

Sure enough, about mid-year 2017 a fairly important member of the staff left the company and when I finally heard about it I thought, "Huh. Well, ok."

Darwin was right. I'd crossed over. And my shoulders no longer hurt.

Still, it took another eighteen months before I knew I could finish this book. It wasn't until I wrote a short piece titled *The Exit* and posted it on my website that I was more certain I had something to say that people would be interested in reading. The most surprising thing for me about writing is that I don't usually know what I'm really writing about until I'm about halfway through with a piece, and such was the case with *The Exit*. I thought I was writing about my husband, but I was really writing about how God used him to prepare me for what is next in my life.

The last three years have been quite an adjustment for me. I caddy for Bill in his PGA tournaments, I'm more available for my family and friends, I have a 12.3 handicap, I have more time to reflect on the successes and failures I experienced owning Paramore Digital and try to make some sense of them. I know for sure that none of it would have happened without the team I had, no matter how imperfect they were. For all their faults, the millennials who tromped through Paramore Digital made a measurable and ultimately positive impact on the company and on me, and there are many of them to thank.

The first leadership team was Amanda Durand Fortune, Brad Haynes, Kate Gallagher and Sheri McCamish. Later Buddy Butler, Josh Miller, Blake Allen, Matt Burch, Ashley Deets Reed, Ben Wilkins and Amy Kaczynski would rotate in and out. We shared triumphs, troubles, drinks and tears. We disagreed then agreed then disagreed again. We struggled through ineffective meetings and celebrated amazing retreats. We supported each other and stabbed each other in the back.

In other words, we were normal.

Thank you all from the bottom of my heart for all you gave to Paramore Digital and to me personally through the years. I hope you are as proud of what we did as I am. And I hope it prepared you for the best years of your life…those which are to come.

As I turned my attention to telling the story of Paramore Digital over the last couple of years and all that we survived, several of the team stepped up to help me sort through and remember the things that needed to be told. In particular Matt Burch and Lizzy Spano who were kind enough to read my scratchy, disorganized notes and reinforce or challenge me. Scott Hutcheson kept telling me to keep going, picking out quirky things that made me think about things differently and reaffirming that what we did at Paramore Digital was special.

I miss my peeps.

There were others who didn't work for Paramore but who urged me on. John Sharpe, Ellen Pryor, and the many people who read early drafts and said, "keep going."

During the final stages of writing I got hooked up with a team of professionals who could make this thing a reality. Honoree Corder taught me everything I know about the publishing process. Tammi Metzler, Terry Stafford, Dino Marino and Julie Allen, the editors and designers, all did their magic to turn words into a book you can hold in your hand.

And then there is my family; disjointed, patched together, better than ever:

Bill Breen, my husband who refocuses me to the important things in life; family, faith, rolling a white ball into a 4-inch hole. And love. Always love.

Barbara Breen, my mother-in-law, the one I was meant to have; resilience, dedication, support and wine. Always wine.

Vera Aderholt, my first granddaughter, my heart; the little eyes that are watching me.

Marie Aderholt Dryden, my daughter, my soul child.

Jason Aderholt, my son, my first, the fulfillment of my childhood dream.

Miriam Paramore, my sister, always supporting me.

Sterl Paramore, my brother, an inspiration.

Jack Paramore, my father, my model.

I stand on the shoulders of giants.

It's amazing how much you cry when you write.

— HIRE ME TO SPEAK —

I built Paramore Digital by speaking at conferences large and small around the world. The most interesting stage I've been on was at the Antonio Pasqualino International Puppet Museum in Palermo, Italy where I spoke to an audience of museum communications professionals from around the world.

Your event could be even more interesting…just give me the microphone!

HIRE ME FOR KEYNOTE PRESENTATIONS ABOUT ANY OF THESE TOPICS:

- Surprising Lessons from 15 Years of Business Ownership
- The Role of the CEO
- Developing a Leadership Team
- Creating a Company Structure That Works
- The Agency/Client Disconnect
- The Top 10 Mistakes Businessowners Make
- The Role of Small Business in America

Email my office at assistant@hannahparamore.com

Connect to me at:
Linkedin.com/hp
Facebook.com/hannahparamore
Instagram.com/hannahparamore59

www.ingramcontent.com/pod-product-compliance
Lightning Source LLC
Chambersburg PA
CBHW071559200326
41519CB00021BB/6807